BECOMING
PERFECT GENTLEMEN

Zach Falconer-Barfield
and Nic Wing

Become the Perfect Gentelman

First published in 2014 by

Panoma Press
48 St Vincent Drive, St Albans, Herts, AL1 5SJ, UK

info@panomapress.com
www.panomapress.com

Book layout by Neil Coe

Printed on acid-free paper from managed forests.

ISBN 978-1-909623-62-0

CONTENTS

ACKNOWLEDGEMENTS

We offer our sincere gratitude to several people who have made this book possible, each have contributed advice, knowledge and support to get this first book to print.

Firstly, the core Perfect Gentleman team, without whom this would have been an exercise in futility, these include Sam Smith and Adam Paciorek.

Our great friends whose advice, guidance and knowledge have steered us through tricky waters: the delightful Lydia Foulkes, Deborah Gayle, Ruairidh Bulger,, and the ever-insightful James Marwood.

Also a big thank you to Tom Swanston, contributor and our resident Editor!

To our lovely collaborators, who have pushed us along the journey, from article writers to guests on our shows, we thank you all.

To the team at Panoma Press, Emma & Mindy foe their extreme patience with us.

Finally and by no means least, our Families, who have put up with us on this Journey to Becoming the Perfect Gentleman.

INTRODUCTION

" A gentleman is one who puts more into the world than he takes out."

George Bernard Shaw

No one forgets the first time he is described as a 'gentleman'. The chest swells with pride; he grows that inch taller, walks with a spring in his step and knows it is a compliment that is rarely thrown around. A gentleman is special.

There was a time when becoming the gentleman was a universal sign of respect, manners and the ideal aspect of the man. Over the last century the Gentleman has become a faded ideal. People question the validity of a concept thought to be based on privilege and nobility. What position does it hold in the modern, fast-paced individualistic society? How does it work in a land of non-conformity and the digital maelstrom? Is there a place for 'colonial hang-overs' in this new global village?

The simple answer is 'Yes, it works'; we have just forgotten the why and neglected the how.

The Gentleman has been around in one form or another for over a thousand years and is nothing if not adaptable and flexible. The Gentleman is an ideal that moves with the times but is based on solid foundations. Like all ideals they are corrupted and the assumptions that are perpetuated are just the 'hang-overs' from bad times of the long history. The gentleman was never supposed to be a misogamist or stuck in his ways, he was built on the sound principles of respect and acceptance.

We decided to correct the course of the 'ideal' and go back to the foundations of what the Gentleman was about, the core values and fundamentals of the building blocks of the Perfect Gentleman.

The Gentleman Advantage

The question we are most asked is, "Why should I learn this stuff? I do not want to be a 'Victorian' man". People often think of the rigid rules, formal dress code and the emotionless man of yesteryear.

The gentleman has changed, adapted and thrived. The Gentleman was constructed as a belief to be the pinnacle of manhood: the perfect mix of martial prowess, spiritual focus and creative endeavour.

Translate that to the modern era, the Gentleman is about becoming a successful businessman, a great leader and romantic figure. The skills that the gentleman possesses in todays world puts them in the top of their fields.

Gentlemen have been perfecting these skills for a thousand years; they are based on pillars of values that have stood the test of time.

Let us look at it from another perspective: Most men have never been taught to shave properly, nor how to choose a suit or clothes that fit them. They are not taught how to behave around ladies, and are lacking many other skills which we men are expected to pick up by osmosis. Would it not be better if there were a resource to help us men?

Why should you become a gentleman? Do you want to become more successful? Earn more money? Get that promotion? Have good and loyal friends? Be respected if not admired by all? Do you want to find that perfect partner? Sweep them off their feet? Keep the flames burning in your love life? Do you want to be the man that everyone talks about?

This is the Gentleman's Advantage.

We wish to give you this advantage.

Making the Gentleman Modern

' Improvise, Adapt, Overcome'

Clint Eastwood 'Heartbreak Ridge

We are exceptionally lucky in building the Perfect Gentleman, though there was a great deal of historical precedent and a few books, it was due to the ideal fading away we had a blank canvas to work on.

The Team wanted from the start to base its Perfect Gentleman on the key values that had stood the test of time and take the best knowledge available to fit within these values. We wanted to make the Gentleman modern, not a Modern Gentleman, and build on all the exceptional work of those that had come before us.

There were several key principles we wished to adhere to:-

1. The Gentleman was based on Values not Rules

2. What we teach are skills and with practice anyone can master them

3. Being a Gentleman is for everyone, not just the wealthy, the nobility, or the elite.

4. Being flexible enough to adapt and improve on anything we teach.

Therefore all that is within this book, any other books, on our website and in our courses, or anything we do, we adhere to these key principles.

In our quest to become The Perfect Gentleman and bring you this work, we have done a huge amount of research, dug through archives, asked our elder gentlemen and sought out experts in their fields to help us with our work. We are always striving to improve and learn.

This Book

This is the first book in our shared journey into 'Becoming the Perfect Gentleman'. It is a detailed but not exhaustive overview of some of the key elements in the toolbox of skills and knowledge that make up the Gentleman. We have selected the key areas in which we feel that the novice can find his way and make a quick and noticeable difference in his world and the world at large. It probably has sections you would not think of and some that you would expect. There are areas that we have not covered, but will do so through other arenas and further book titles.

We advise you to quickly read the whole book and then pick the sections you would like to work on first and that resonate with you, master them and then move on to the other sections. Please feel free to look at the resources and links on the website to help you. Remember, little easy wins build confidence and create a solid footing.

It is about stepping into the carriage on the first train to the destination of The Gentleman. We know that you will perhaps want to take different paths, different modes of transport and add different elements to your experience. We welcome this variety and aim to make your journey easy and spectacular.

The Rise of the Gentleman

We are here to prove that the Gentleman has not been forgotten, it might have faded and been disparaged but it has proved its worth as a concept and as a breeding ground for successful men time and time again.

We believe that it is time. The twilight is over and men should reclaim the Gentleman as the way forward. The better way, the happy medium between the rampaging Alpha Male and the foppish metrosexual is the way of the Gentle-Man. Let us stand up to be counted and show that we as Gentleman can make the world a better more respectful, stylish and gentlemanly place... even if we have to do it one man at a time.

A Short History of the Gentleman

> " *Study history, study history. In history lies all the secrets of statecraft.* "
>
> **Sir Winston Churchill**

The Ideal of the Gentleman has lasted for thousands of years. It is a concept that has been moulded over centuries, admirably stood the test of time and only faltered occasionally. However, after almost a century of being underutilised and mismanaged, the gentleman is once again on the rise and we are here to help him.

Our focus through this brief history is on the British Gentleman and how he came to being, his rise over the ages and how he has fallen to where he is today.

The Ancient Gentleman

It could be comfortably said that the ideal was found in the mists of the ancient worlds of Greece, Rome, India and China. A ruling class would admire the skill at arms of its men, but it was certain tribes and countries that began to admire other skills, such as the ability to be a great orator, create art, display generosity and show compassion.

This ancient proto-gentleman had physical skills; he could ride a horse, shoot a bow and wield a sword against his enemies. But he was also mentally astute, able to hold discourse on politics, admire what is beautiful and have a desire for knowledge.

Plato, the great Greek philosopher, wrote of exactly these gentlemen when he talked of his guardians of the state.

Our early Chinese gentlemen were warrior monks practising martial arts and working on their spiritual growth, or their Indian cousins, working on mental, physical and spiritual training.

Early warriors not only developed martial skills, but also had other attributes in the quest for bettering themselves.

Sadly, it fell away in Europe and only religious men ended up being the educated ones.

The Dark Ages & First Battles

There were certainly no gentlemen in Britain to begin with. The Roman conquerors brought with them ancient aesthetics of grace and skill, which fell under the axe of the Vikings, Saxons and other violent aggressors. Life was of little value in those wild days: the conqueror would take all: your life, your wife and anything else that would take his fancy.

One of the last kings of this period, Harold, was a moral king and a true early gentleman. He was highly regarded by his subjects, and even offered his traitorous brother a way out and redemption at his penultimate battle. Harold was the king who successfully defended England from the Vikings at Stamford Bridge and then only a few days later almost succeeded in defeating the Norman invaders, led by William the Conqueror.

One can discuss what might have happened had Harold won that day in 1066 but what did happen was the foundation of manners in Britain.

The conquering armies of Europe began to realise that developing an element of good behaviour and some form of moral conduct was much more effective than brutality in subduing the natives. In Britain, William and his two hundred Norman families could not hope to run all of England with just brute force; there would have been a quick revolution.

These early instances of manners came to be an effective diplomatic and political tool for ruling, as the British Empire perfected many centuries later.

Good Manners are infectious and more effective than having rowdy, drunken armed men over to dinner and worrying about whether you might loose your head and cause a small war over a perceived slight. This code of behaviour became the way to mitigate the problem of loosing good men and halting revolution.

Another thing that heavily influenced the birth of the Gentleman was the Crusades. Actually it was not the Crusades themselves, but the lessons learned by the returning knights who had experienced a whole new world and absorbed the culture of their foreign counterparts with whom they had interacted. They learned that warriors could also be poets, artists and have skills outside the martial, and even more than that, they where expected to. This is clearly demonstrated in the film 'The 13th Warrior', in which Antonio Banderas' character plays the warrior poet and ambassador to the Caliph of Baghdad, who ends up with a group of Vikings each learning from each other. It is also demonstrated in the film "The Kingdom of Heaven" on how the Crusades can affect someone of that period.

It was in this dark period of history, when the paragon of Knighthood and one of the true founders of the Chivalry code was said to operate; King Arthur, and his Knights of the roundtable.

The legendary Arthur and the tales of derring-do and moral guidance performed by him and his Knights, were made famous by Geoffrey of Monmouth's 'Historia Regum Britiania', which was written much later in the 12th Century. Now the historical accuracy of Arthur's actual existence might be in doubt, but the effect of his actions on the history of Britain and the foundations of the Gentleman are momentous.

In these tales, Arthur and his Knights exemplified what was written down not long before in Geoffrey's book, the Code of Chivalry.

The Code of Chivalry

If one thing and one thing alone could be said to be the foundation of what it is to be a gentleman, then that thing would be the Knights Code of Chivalry.

During this period of time, the Knight was coming out of his dark past as an aggressive killing warrior. He was beginning to temper this aggressive side with a moral system, which, though heavily influenced by religion, was not a religious code.

Though several codes existed since the 8th Century, none were written down, they were oral conditions.

The Knights Code of Chivalry was finally put into written form in the 'Song of Roland' (Le Chanson de Roland), in the mid-12th Century. It told the tales of Count Roland, who served with the great Emperor Charlemagne in the 8th Century. This poem was amazingly popular and made into many, many manuscripts, which spread across Europe.

The Code of Chivalry, according to the Song of Roland, is as follows:-

To fear God and maintain His Church

To serve the liege lord in valour and faith

To protect the weak and defenceless

To give succour to widows and orphans

To refrain from the wanton giving of offence

To live by honour and for glory

To despise pecuniary reward

To fight for the welfare of all

To obey those placed in authority

To guard the honour of fellow knights

To eschew unfairness, meanness and deceit

To keep faith

At all times to speak the truth

To persevere to the end in any enterprise begun

To respect the honour of women

Never to refuse a challenge from an equal

Never to turn the back upon a foe

Of these, two thirds are related to conduct that had nothing to do with combat. This code was reaffirmed in oaths and vows committed to within religious ceremonies, enabling a man to become a Knight.

The Code was a changing set of rules and was refined over the course of the medieval period. For example; the Duke of Burgundy came up with a set of words that describes for what seemed to him to embody the virtues of a knight.

Faith

Charity

Justice

Sagacity

Prudence

Temperance

Resolution

Truth

Liberality

Diligence

Hope

Valour

These values and codes are the foundations upon which the gentleman was formed.

It is interesting to think that only one other culture outside Medieval Europe developed a written code of conduct for its warriors that balanced martial prowess with the skills of court and romance. That culture was that of Japan and the Samurai warrior's code of Bushido, an even more rigid code of conduct than the one of Europe.

The Virtues of Bushido

Courage

Benevolence

Respect

Honesty

Honour

Loyalty

Rectitude (Righteousness)

Fascinatingly, the Japanese code of conduct had the same core principles as the European code, and it has also lasted the test of time. It is amazing to think that two island cultures, which were on opposite sides of the globe, shared such values.

Chaucer & The Rudimentary Gentleman

In England, the language of court and nobility was French and the dominant language of literature alongside Latin. Chaucer wrote in the vernacular English and his writings, especially 'The Canterbury Tales', were widely popular.

What makes him such an impact in the History of the Gentleman is that he unified the country with a common language and gave the whole of England a unified identity.

At the same time, a member of the English court stood up and asked why the affairs of state and those of law should not now be conducted in English. Henceforward they were, and it was not long before the commoner and the king were speaking the same language.

"Being good with a sword and perhaps a bow"; quotes Chaucer; "sing a song; understood the law; hold a conversation; the ability to read and perhaps even playing football with the men; keeping up the Chivalry traditions and values." These were the basics, and their essence did not change for the next 600 years.

England was now united by a language and a code of conduct. The rudimentary gentleman of today was born.

The Books and Guides

With each century the scale of accomplishments, and what was required by society's code of conduct, grew higher and higher. It became more and more challenging and it was no wonder that the by the 16th century some form of guidance into this world was needed.

If one book could be seen to influence the perception of the gentleman in England, it was 'The Book of the Courtier' (1528), a 'bestseller' across Europe written by an Italian, Baldassare Castiglione.

This book addressed the constitution of the perfect courtier. It is set as a series of fictional conversations between the courtiers of an Italian Duke, discussed over several evenings and covering what the perfect gentleman of court should be. They concluded that he should have a cool mind; good voice (in other words able to speak eloquently); proper bearing and gesture; good knowledge of classics, culture and fine art, but also he must have the warrior spirit.

It is widely recognised that the English translation of the book, released in 1561, had a profound effect on the conception of the English Gentleman.

It is amusing to think that the first English Guide on being a Gentleman, written by an Englishman was published 400 years ago. Richard Braithwaite, an English poet, author and soldier, wrote his guide to conduct and manners, The English Gentleman (1630) and followed it up with The English Gentlewoman (1631).

His guide to being the better English gentleman covered such areas as Youth, Disposition, Education, Vocation, Recreation, Acquaintance, Moderation and Perfection.

As the world grew increasingly complex, it became obvious that people needed guides and to be reminded of the core principles with which to go about their daily business.

The Renaissance Gentleman

The Elizabethan & Jacobean Gentleman of the late sixteenth and early seventeenth centuries was in an unenviable position. England was on the rise, with a powerful navy, global trade and great discoveries coming to the fore.

It was the age of Shakespeare, who gave voice to the cross section of English men and women, everything from the nobility and courtesy of Henry V, to the noble gestures of romantic heroes such as Romeo. Across every walk of life he showed how the Gentleman should behave, and the consequences of his actions when he did not.

The Great Cultural renaissance, which had been slowly sweeping across Europe, had reached its climax. The historical gentleman were being rediscovered, the Greek and Roman philosophy was reborn in the words of Thomas Moore and Niccolo Machiavelli. Art, science and learning had become democratised thanks to the printing press and the rise of education establishments.

One of the lesser-known but fascinating gentlemen of this period was James Crichton, also known as the Admirable Crichton. He encapsulated what all men of the period aspired to be, and some would say he was the complete man. He was certainly a rarity and a prodigy. By the age of twenty he could converse and write in twelve languages, he was a skilled fencer, horseman, singer, musician, speaker and he was noted for being not only charming and mannered but also handsome.

Whilst studying in Paris, he was challenged by the French professors from the College de Navarre to answer any question in either the sciences or arts. He agreed and even said they could ask in any of the languages he knew. It is said over the course of a very, very long day that he bested the French Scholars. They found no question he could not answer, no matter how obscure. It is said he repeated the feat in Italy, not once but twice.

He came to a tragic end, as recounted by his biographer Sir Thomas Urquhart, when he went to Mantua and served as tutor to the

Duke's son. Sadly, the son was jealous and late one night, masked and with accomplices attacked Crichton. He bested all, but when the ringleader revealed himself to be his friend and employer's son, James Crichton dropped to his knee and presented his sword to the hotheaded son. The son took the sword and killed Crichton. He died before his 22nd birthday. He was the total gentleman, even in his last action.

During this period 'Britain', as it was now to be known, thanks to James I, was a rich and diverse country, which harboured many cultures and influences. The ideal of the gentleman was being refined by commerce, knowledge and travel.

The Fop, The Dandy & Style

As the gentleman moved through from through the expansion and glory of the Elizabethan and Jacobean periods, the world began to change.

The empire was expanding, cities were expanding, and knowledge was expanding. Commercialism was rising and war was happening all over the world. The gentleman was becoming a part of the fabric of society.

Almost like today the gentleman was split between an ornate, colourful, parakeet of a man and the dour taciturn military-type figure. The gentleman had lost his thrust. At one end of the spectrum were the fops, early metro-sexuals that primped and preened, who were incapable of serious thought and were often mocked. At the other end of the spectrum were hard working, dour and rule-driven men, such as the country squires of the period.

A great example of the dichotomy of the Gentleman was the fictional character hero Sir Percival Blakeney, known as The Scarlet Pimpernel; on the surface a fop, but underneath a man of action and daring. He, and others from the piles of romantic fiction penned by such authors as Jane Austen, hinted not so subtly that this type of man was missing or at the very least rare. When would the dashing gentleman return?

Some men were striving to change the male. One man did more for men's fashion and the ideal of that arena as far as the Gentleman is concerned, and his name was George 'Beau' Brummell. He almost single-handedly changed men's fashion, bringing about the change that would eventually become men's style as we know it today.

Beau Brummell, was born in London and raised to be a gentleman. His natural character and wit made him many friends and quite a few enemies. What Beau did so well was clothing. He changed the foppish fashions of the past into simple styles, caring about the shape and cut of the clothing, and thinking about contrasting colours. He was certainly the influence for the modern suit and necktie. His style and trend became known as Dandyism, though now the word has attached to it connotations of fashion and extremes, it really was the cornerstone of style.

Brummell's statue resides in Jermyn Street, London, overlooking this area known for men's tailoring, making sure that the man is known for style, never fashion.

The Victorian Gentleman & the Empire

When someone thinks or mentions a gentleman, one thinks of the Victorian Ideal. This image of the ramrod straight, immaculately dressed and formally mannered, wax moustached man is the first image that springs to mind. The era was one that stressed morality, self-restraint and proper behaviour, rules abound. Without a shadow of a doubt the gentleman came into its own during the Victorian age; the Empire and the Gentleman rose together during this period.

What constituted the Victorian Gentleman? It was an amalgam of all the previous influences that had taken us to this point. Style and grooming played a formable part in the life of the gentleman. He was expected to be properly dressed, which included a suit of jacket and trousers, generally a cravat and waistcoat and when outdoors a hat. He was expected to be of exceptional hygiene, a gentleman was to be seen not smelt, and indeed a little perfume was suggested. Manners and Etiquette were of paramount importance, a gentleman was expected to treat every person he encountered correctly and properly. There was pressure never to be the slightest bit insulting. He was to adhere to the qualities of chivalry, courtesy, courage and kindness. He was expected also to be honourable and brave, to protect those around him from ruffians and louts. If that was not enough to be going on with, he was expected to be financially savvy and seek to always better himself. All in all, the gentleman's plate was a full one.

However, the gentleman was to be no longer associated with the wealthy or the nobility, but with the distinctions of education and manners. A gentleman could come from anywhere and indeed did. Because of this there arose a huge swathe of guidebooks on etiquette, manners and conduct for men and ladies, with such titles as 'On Deportment', 'Young Lady's Friend', 'Good Manners', 'The Young Man's Guide' and 'Manners for Men'.

In fact, by the mid part of the 1800s, being a gentleman had become almost a religion, the ideal had grown to appeal to all, but it was a religion without supernatural leanings.

Indeed there were now a plethora of 'seminaries', known as 'public schools', which educated and taught boys turning them into young gentleman. At the start of the century there were only nine such schools, but by the end of the same century there were nearly three hundred. These public schools harked back once again to our Greco-Roman proto-gentleman, they wanted to create men who had sound moral principles, gentlemanly conduct, intellectual aptitude and an ability to play games (which was a substitute for combat skills). One of the main reasons for the growth of these institutions is the demand for roles to be filled as the Empire and commercialisation grew across the world. There were Colonial Governors in Australia, Judges in India, Army Officers in the Sudan and Schoolmasters in Canada.

This was the Imperial century for Great Britain, the influence spread across the world, it held sway to about one-fifth of the world's population and approximately a quarter of the world's land mass. Therefore its cultural legacy ran through the very fibre of the world and the reason to this day that the ideal of the gentleman is fixed in the mind's eye of the world.

This was helped by various cultural items, which spread these ideals across the world. Literature was full of tales of gentlemen or men that aspired to those ideals, such as: Sir Walter Scott, who wrote of the heroics of historical characters such as *Ivanhoe* or *Rob Roy*; Charles Dickens, who wrote often of people showing the qualities of gentleman in such works as *A Tale of Two Cities* or Great Expectations; or the romantic gentleman displayed in the works of the Brontë sisters. As the century drew to a close the icon of the adventuring gentleman was displayed in such fictional characters as Arthur Conan Doyle's *Sherlock Holmes*, Rudyard Kipling's *Kim* or H. Rider Haggard's Alan *Quartermain*. These gentlemen not only acted heroically, they did so with style.

Literature was not the only cultural export of the Empire; the gentleman sportsman was hitting or kicking balls across the world. Football, Rugby, Cricket, Tennis, and Golf spread in popularity, rules were written and the first great tournaments were held during this century. All of these sports were played and exported by gentlemen and therefore the ideals of sportsmanship and gentlemanly behaviour were forever interlinked. The Victorians did a most excellent job of making rough games without rules into a moral and spiritual pastime that could foster feelings of solidarity and making all feel like gentlemen.

Therefore, by the end of the 19th Century, the gentleman abounded in deed, in imagination and in the hearts and minds of every British man and many others around the globe. The gentleman had truly become linked with Britain and the image of the British gentleman, resplendent in a suit, able to discourse on any subject and generally capable of most things, whilst at the same time able to make all feel at ease.

The Gilded Fall

" Unseen in the background, Fate was quietly slipping lead into the boxing-glove. "

P.G. Wodehouse, Very Good, Jeeves!

From the Edwardian era and over the first four decades of the 20th century, the gentleman fell from the giddy heights of Victorian achievement to the mud and disdain of Post War austerity. A number of factors came to play which changed the gentleman and his ideal: firstly, the difference between rich and poor and the changes that were coming; secondly, the two World Wars and their impact; thirdly, the rise of equality; and finally, the breaking up of the British Empire and the rise of the new powers.

The difference between rich and poor was exceptional, perhaps a third of the population lived in deep poverty, though there were great strides being done to change this, there was a seething undercurrent. The country was full of strikes, radical attacks on the Houses of Parliament, and the belief that revolution was imminent.

Then there was the indifference of the 'haves' to the 'have nots'. Being a gentleman was seen as an elitist thing. In fact the portrayal of the feckless gentleman idiots, by such authors as P. G. Wodehouse, highlighted the return to foppishness of the Regency gentleman. The so-called 'Long Weekend' between the World Wars, was full of excess, parties and exuberance but also a time of the Wall Street Crash and the Great Depression, the world was changing and some kept dancing.

Some of the biggest social changes happened due to the two World Wars, and several of these affected the gentleman. The First World War destroyed a generation of young men, especially a great many who had gone through those gentlemanly institutions the 'Public Schools'. These men where bred for the playing fields of Eton, not the battlefields of the Somme. The men in charge, who were the elite gentlemen, had made some drastic and tragic mistakes and the perception of the stature of the gentleman was waning. During both wars, the officer class, which was predominantly made up of the 'gentleman' lived and died for probably the first time en masse with the general soldier. This living 'cheek by jowl' changed the social barriers as well as the many more people from the ranks being promoted to officers. Another destabilising factor was the radically different American troops of the Second World War and their new and challenging attitudes to the 'stuck up Brits' and their Victorian behaviour.

The combination of the decimation of a whole stratum of men, the breaking down of the class barriers due to death and new 'American' thinking, was rapidly bringing about the fall of the Gentleman.

Women were changing the face of the world, they had come from behind the curtain and demanded recognition, the right to vote and, due to the wars, an equal footing on the career path. They achieved these things, rightly so, and the attitudes of the Victorian stiff rules of morals and etiquette were shaken at their foundations and men began to be unsure of their footing on the path to chivalry.

By the end of the Second World War, the British Empire was ripped to shreds and the gentleman was equally as tattered. The strong moral and formal ways of Great Britain had been swept aside by the effervescence of the rising American juggernaut and the frosty calm of the Soviet Union. The British global cultural influence was in danger of being eradicated.

The gentleman had almost become a figure of ridicule and synonymous with idleness, empire and privilege.

It is a drastic misconception to think that the period was devoid of gentlemen. That is certainly not the case, gentlemen existed in all forms. The selfless heroes of the World Wars, to the gentleman pioneers of aviation, exploration and innovation and the tycoons of business, were at every turn. The cultural impact of the Gentleman was being exploited by the new blooming Film Industry, it was safe to say he was not a dead ideal, but he was certainly a fallen idol.

The Lost Generations

" We didn't start the fire; No we didn't light it, But we tried to fight it "

Billy Joel

Post war Britain was a very different world and not one where the Gentleman could find his footing; he was fading away, becoming a fictional tool and a distant ideal. The counter culture and social revolution that exploded in the late 1950s and all the way through the 1960s brought about the period of excess, the fall of such things as sexism, racism and colonial power.

Liberalism, Commercialism, Individualism, Feminism, Globalisation, the rise of American culture, international corporations, the speed of technological advance and so many things have happened in the last 70 years, and all of it has changed the role of the male in society.

The gentleman faded and was replaced by various other forms as men struggled to find a role and an identity. Spanning from one end of the spectrum was the Metro-sexual, the modern fop, all the way to the Alpha Male, in the same vein as the pre-code of chivalry warriors. There are many other points along the spectrum, but the one that has stuck around and influenced the last two decades is the 'lad culture', which is a drastic backlash to feminism, where men are dominated by drinking, watching sport and sex. It has been the key cultural male influence with all the male magazines guiding their readers to this lifestyle.

The skills of the gentleman that were so highly regarded in previous centuries had been deemed outdated or merely attributes of fictional heroes. Skills such as the ability to romance and woo, to defend the weak, to act with compassion, to understand style and be groomed, had fallen off the 'To Do' lists of busy parents, the curriculum of schools, and were deemed a disadvantage in the ruthless business word. And yet, these repudiated skills are held in esteem in the cultural world, once again showing that the need was called for, as in the previous centuries when they faded for a time. In romance films the hero sweeps his lady off her feet, the action hero saves the puppy and the child from the clutches of death; the dashing gentleman thief only steals from those that are shown to be villains. The Gentleman is a hero, which should not be reserved for fiction or the occasional compliment.

So for the rest of the 20th Century and into the 21st Century the gentleman had lost his way. He was still held up as an occasional ideal but now one that had flaws and even a dark underbelly.

The Rise of the New Gentleman

There is a feeling that the pendulum has swung too far away from the centre. There is a swell building in the sea of masculinity that the Gentleman needs to return. The male is having an identity crisis, confused by old brutish stereotypes of masculinity or waspish, primped, overly feminized males, combined with a global multi-cultural world, and gender roles that have not yet settled into their new paradigm; the male is in a state of flux.

You can hear it with the talk of the lack of manners that is spoken throughout the mainstream media. You can see it with the people demanding a return to style over fashion through their posts in Social Media. You can feel it pulse through the populous that a lack of compassion and propensity for greed in business and life will not be tolerated. You can touch the pulse of women, who are fed up with a lack of romance in their relationships. You can taste in the air that the skills that once were a daily lesson for all men are ready to be picked up again.

This brief history of the Gentleman has shown that it has been an ideal and has survived for a millennium because the core principles work. The skills and trappings have changed over time to accommodate the world's progress but the core values and principles have not changed, but have instead been refined over time. The ideal of the Gentleman has stood the test of time, it is still held up as a pinnacle of masculinity but the skills have been forgotten, the generation that could have taught us is rapidly passing away. We need to retain these skills and pass them on to future generations.

The gentleman is ready to once again claim the space that sits between the fop/metrosexual and the lad/alpha male. It is time for us men to step up and reclaim the Gentle-Man and reinstill the true meaning of chivalry to the world. We are here to make the Gentleman modern, to make the world more respectful, more confident, more stylish, more mannered and we urge you to help us by changing yourself and becoming that one Gentleman that makes a difference.

THE CORE OF THE GENTLEMAN

" A gentleman would be ashamed should his deeds not match his words."

Confucius

The Gentleman Ideal

The Gentleman is an Ideal not just a stylish three-piece suit or perfect table manners. We believe that to become the Perfect Gentleman not only do you need to learn the skills that make you excel but the mindset and values that can help you reach the pinnacle of success in all aspects of life.

Of all the skills and principles that can be found in this book, we believe that this chapter and these core values will be the ones that change you most into Becoming the Perfect Gentleman. We are aware of many men that may wear a bespoke suit and will steal every penny from your pocket and the devilish charmer that whisks women into bad relationships. These are not gentlemen. They may have the trappings, but a true gentleman is one who starts and ends his journey from within.

The Ideal of the Gentleman has been around for some time, as we read in the previous chapter. It was first written down in the 'Song of Roland' and has been modified over the course of time and its principles can be found in the Samurai's code of Bushido and through the behaviour expected of a military officer in any country in the world and even in such documents as the Declaration of Independence. These ideals are all around us but they have been watered down, misplaced, dismissed and even plain forgotten.

These values do exist in the hearts of many, but have been forgotten or buried in the misguided belief that they do not fit in today's world. We are here to bring them to the forefront of people's hearts, minds and spirits.

This Core of the Gentleman is made up of a set of values, which we have distilled from various sources, discussions and historical references. We believe these are the fundamental principles by which the modern Gentleman should live.

These various values, in different ways, give a sense of stability direction and purpose in a world that seems to be inherently lacking in such.

But let us start by understanding what values are and how we can change them.

' Believe you can, Believe you can't – either way you are right.'

Henry Ford

What are Values?

Without values and beliefs, a moral compass if you will, we are a rudderless boat in the sea of life. Generally we do not spend time thinking about our values and beliefs. They seem to have appeared out of the air, or we feel that they are based on elements of how we are raised and people's values are fixed, immutable and solid. Not very much of that is true. One thing is very true; beliefs are exceptionally important, they are the things that start wars.

Beliefs are, as Antony Robbins puts it, "Any guiding principle, dictum, faith or passion that can provide meaning and direction in life." We develop these beliefs through our cultural setting, our community or family, our social circle and through our interactions with the world.

Some beliefs are universal or pure, such as the Sun will rise, apples will fall from trees and water will boil if heated. These are the way things are. Though some beliefs are judgements, our position on the way things should be, these are our evaluations based on our personal beliefs, or our Values.

The Values that we have are those personal individual beliefs about what is most vital to you. These are the rudders of what is good or bad, right or wrong. These are the navigation points we use to guide us across the sea of life.

We do not really think about our values or beliefs, thus the 'belief' that they come from the air. Often we are unaware of our values until we encounter people with different values and our own are challenged.

Some values are positive and helpful and some are negative and repressive. For example, we have a friend, who is exceptionally negative about his attractiveness to the opposite sex. His sets of beliefs are that because of his race, his lack of height and his relative lack of wealth, women are not interested in him. These, as you can imagine are not very positive, and because of these beliefs he does not try or pushes potential suitors away.

Changing Values

The question is - can you change your beliefs and values? Yes, you can. There are probably a number of things that you used to believe in that you now do not; Father Christmas? The Tooth Fairy? The Easter Bunny? Our perceptions and our beliefs change with time, with experiences and with encounters with others. Who has not heard of people having sudden conversions to religious faiths? These are belief changes and can occur in a moment or develop over time.

Luckily for us, there are now techniques to change our beliefs quickly. These techniques, such as Neuro-linguistic Programming, Cognitive Behavioural Therapy and others, can rapidly change you from one position to another. The key thought is YOUR willingness to change. As with everything, YOUR desire to change is the key motivating factor and the only way.

So let us give you a couple of ways to start your belief change. Firstly, to live 'As If' ,or 'Believe it to be so and it will become so'. It is now a proven fact that your body goes through the same physical reactions to stimuli if you only imagine that the thing occurs. Sports people now do huge visualisation exercises to stimulate their responses to situations that they may find themselves in. So, the first step is to deeply feel that it is so. If you want to be determined and focused, believe it to be so. Keep believing every day, tell people that you are, look every day in the mirror and affirm that you are determined. Be proactive, take small steps that help you secure wins and every day you will find that it starts to embed into your being. As the famous Boxer, Muhammad Ali once said, "If my mind can conceive it and my heart can believe it, then I can achieve it."

Secondly, use your physical body to engage your mind and emotions. Amy Cuddy, who is a professor at Harvard, has done some amazing research into how your body language can influence who you are. Let us try a little experiment, put a big huge goofy grin on your face. Yes a really large silly one. Are you doing it? Good. Now try and have a negative thought, about anything. It is really, really difficult to do. In fact whenever there is stress around, put on a big smile and your emotions will change. Professor Cuddy found that by engaging in some physical stances, what she calls 'power poses' for just two minutes you can significantly change, not only others impressions of us but our own internal workings. One example is to place your hands on your hips and to spread your legs, adopting the 'Superman' pose, if you will. By doing these just two minutes a day, you can change everything. Combine this with your visualisation from before and double those effects. Please got to www.theperfectgentleman.tv/BPGresources for the link to her TED talk, which goes into much more detail and shows the poses.

Thirdly on our rapid belief change is affirmations. This is a somewhat dated method now, but if you do not have access to people or you want to get started now this is another quick way to promote change. Affirmations are basically phrases or sayings that imbue the values or beliefs that you want to achieve. For example, "with everyday and every-way, I am becoming more determined", "I am the chivalrous knight", "I respect all, starting with myself". Feel free to make up your own. The trick is to make them positive, present tense and focused.

Now combine them, with your power pose, your visualisation and you have triple the change firing through your mind.

These are a few quick ways to help you fast track your belief changes. Please try these on your own, we also recommend either seeking out a qualified practitioner near you or come to our website and we have some products and coaching links that can help you change your beliefs and mindset rapidly.

(www.theperfectgentleman.tv/BPGrescources/)

We have discussed how you may change, now let us delve deeper into what values we want to instill in you, naturally they are gentlemanly ones.

The Golden Principle – Respect

' Seek first to understand, then be understood.'

Stephen R Covey

We have a core value at The Perfect Gentleman, which we believe holds everything else we do together, from which all the other values stem.

Re-spect (definition edited)

- *esteem for or a sense of the worth or excellence of a person, a personal quality or ability or something considered as a manifestation of a personal quality or ability.*

- *Proper acceptance or courtesy*

- *To show regard or consideration for*

- *To hold in esteem or honour*

Respect is something that has been slowly eroded over the last few decades. It can be seen in so many different ways, let us talk about some examples.

A friend of ours is a football referee; he is neither in the Premiership nor in any of the top divisions but he gives up his weekends to help. In his time he has been shouted at; sworn at; had some truly horrible things said about him and his family; spat at; threatened and even physically abused. Simply put, this is appalling. We have seen it on the top-flight professional football fields. Where is the respect for his authority?

In another conversation one of the team was having with a fireman, he was telling a story of how he was taking early retirement because he was fed up of being sent out on false or ridiculous calls and thus risking the lives of others by doing so. This is a man who risks his own life to rescue others and is fed up with some people's lack of respect for his calling.

Lastly, one of our personal annoyances: watching couples out on a date. The lady has made an effort: she has dressed up; done her make up; put on her heels and dabbed her perfume. She is looking fabulous. The man she is with, on the other hand, looks like he has just stepped off the couch after playing video games for the last two days. There is no respect for the date, the lady, himself or indeed the relationship.

We need to change these thought patterns and beliefs, and instill the value of respect, as you will read in the next section.

We are not for one second saying people should not question or challenge the status quo or not take up legitimate problems. What we are wishing to do is to make you think about the manner in which it is done. It is sometimes done at best with a lack of thought and at worst with hatred and malice of forethought.

We are all human and we all make mistakes and we all loose our cool. But next time, take a moment and think about how the other person will feel, think about their job, what they want and think how you would wish to be treated. We are all heroes in our own movie.

If we all had Respect for one another and the world at large, this world would be a truly special place.

The Three Levels of Respect

What we have defined at The Perfect Gentleman is that all our values are based on 3 levels. There are three levels of Respect and these coincide with the other 12 values as they fit in to each of these levels.

The levels are Internal or the 'Me' level, the second is the External or the 'Others' Level, and thirdly is the Greater Good or the 'World' level.

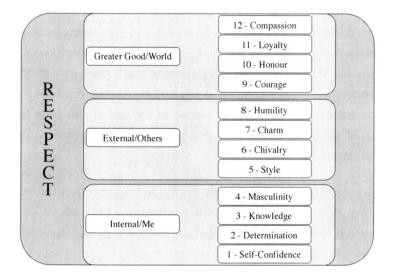

Me/Internal

The first level of Respect is that shown to oneself. What do we mean by respecting oneself? It is simple, as is most things. Are you respecting your body, your mind and your spirit?

Do you respect your body to eat well and healthy? Are you taking exercise to maintain it in good condition? Are you making sure you get enough sleep and taking care of the body that you have?

This has become a massive problem, so much so that now governments are trying to regulate against obesity and other related health problems. We have forgotten to show respect for our own bodies and take care of them ourselves. We should look after this one body we have, respect it.

We are in a knowledge world, information is at our fingertips and everywhere, we can read, watch and learn much easier than at any other time in history. Our minds need to be stimulated; we are not saying everyone should pursue formal education. What we are affirming is that to respect the mind is to engage it and use it. Learn new things, have discussions with friends and even strangers about things that matter. You will find that your brain is more capable than you thought and you can achieve so much more than maybe you realise. You are certainly doing well by reading this book. If you want more, the resource section at the end of this book has lists of the books we researched to bring you this information. You can start there.

The one thing that most people neglect to respect is their spiritual being. Whether you are religious, spiritual or a pure atheist, your internal sprit needs to be respected. We need to take time with ourselves and do things that make us internally happy. That could be as simple as reading a great fiction book, talking a long walk through the woods, going on holiday, going to church, spending time in prayer, meditation or thought.

Whatever it is, you need to spend time with you, making you a better and more rounded person.

This level of respect is the one that you can affect the most and is also the one that affects all the others the most. Think about this, if you are fit, healthy, well read, and spiritually at peace, what a more outstanding person you would be.

External/Others

" You can make more friends in two months by becoming interested in other people than you can in two years by trying to get other people interested in you. "

Dale Carnegie

The external level of respect starts with those closest to us: our partners, our family, and our friends. Then extends beyond that to our colleagues, our business associates and even down to people we encounter in our everyday lives.

By showing respect to those closest to us we show them that we care and we are interested in them and their lives. This extends to everyone we encounter, by showing respect we will earn it.

Our loved ones, family and friends, we know should deserve our respect. The question is do we show it, do we take time to listen to them, to spend time with them and respect their thoughts and feelings amongst other things.

This has become a 'me first' world. In Singapore they even have a word for it - 'Kiasu' (a Hokkien word) it loosely translates as 'fear of loosing'. In fact for many years it was actively encouraged, but now even the Singapore government has seen the errors of its ways and started 'politeness campaigns'. What they realised is that politeness and respect is a social glue, which makes societies function smoothly. Pushing, shoving and a lack of gratitude makes for a difficult place to live and work, especially in our ever more populated world.

This social glue has been put to one side for greed, speed, selfishness and short term thinking, to name a few of these negative driving forces. It is about time that respect for those around us is at the forefront of our choices and consciousness. Remember how you feel, when you see the smile on someone's face by being polite, using their name, helping someone with luggage up that flight of stairs, or any other small gesture of respect. Remember this when engaging with anyone that you encounter.

Greater Good/ World

' A butterfly can flap its wings in one part of the world and cause a hurricane in another part of the world.'

Edward Lorenz

The world is now a very small place and growing increasingly interconnected. This is not just true of technology but also how we interact with the world around us. One cannot deny that we are affecting the planet and not always for the better. We can make lists upon lists of things that we have had an affect on, causing problems, changes and destruction. We are not saying that we are not doing fabulous things, but we have to think about the consequences for our actions and their impact in the greater context.

We have to Respect the planet that we live in and the interactions with the world at large. As with everything, start small, such as to throw your rubbish in a bin and not the street, remember to recycle, think about that business decision and the impact it will have on others.

Since commercial space travel has not been made feasible and we have not colonised other worlds, we need to work on this one and with the people on it. It is not just for this generation but the ones that are coming that we need to engender this level of respect.

The Twelve Values

The Perfect Gentleman's reinvigoration of the core values for the modern man are listed below. Although they are ordered and listed in levels, we believe that these values are all equal and can be worked on in whichever order that suits the individual. Some will be easy and strike to the core and others will require diligence and work.

Remember, Respect is the key value, and if there is one value you take to heart, then do that.

First Level – Internal

The four values here are the ones that are cultivated internally but have exceptional external benefits.

1. Self Confidence

One of the keys to success in life and especially romance and business is self-confidence, though it is sometimes the hardest value to grasp.

Belief in yourself is being comfortable in your own skin and abilities, but with the knowledge that you can always learn and do better.

Sometimes, it is not easy to find this value; it is one that takes some time to build.

There was a time when our own 1st Gentleman was unconfident, friendless and unwilling to step outside. He never believed that he would stand on stage in front of thousands of people, be able to influence others and have the confidence to run his own business.

As we mentioned earlier in the changing values section, there are now skills and techniques that are available to you to help with this. Our own 1ˢᵗ Gentleman used them to great affect. Just remember that small wins, rapidly build to bigger wins and greater confidence.

A Gentleman's Hint:

If you need a confidence boost; Stand up straight and tall, place your hands comfortably on your hips and start to breath deeply, through your nose only and with each breath start to feel the confidence flow through you. Do this for one or two minutes and see what a difference it makes.

For more information & instructions head to www.theperfectgentleman.tv/BPGresources

2. Determination

> ' If you wanna be the best, and you wanna beat the rest, dedication's what you need... '

Roy Castle

If you ask most sportspeople, entrepreneurs and other highly successful people, the one key common factor in their success is determination. They can phrase it as determination, dedication or perseverance, but the ability to never stop or give up is paramount.

The tales abound of men and women, who have overcome fantastic odds to succeed. Whether these challenges are financial, physical, mental or any other disadvantages, they have had the ferocious determination and discipline to climb their own personal Mount Everest.

A gentleman's determination to succeed, whether in personal challenges, business, romance or life as a whole, is a value that inspires admiration. The ability to keep going when the road is tough and full of challenges makes him a better man.

A Gentleman's Hint:

Each morning when you wake up, write down one small thing that you want to achieve that day. (do the shopping, make that sales call, write your profile update). Make sure you do it and then cross it off your list at night. Do it for a week and then add a second thing a day the next week, do the thing and cross it off. Continue adding each week for a month and then see what you have achieved.

---

3. Knowledge

' The Pen is mightier than the sword'

Edward Bulwer-Lytton

Whether education is formal or informal, knowledge has great power. It has the power to change worlds, influence groups and raise the lowliest person to the greatest heights.

A gentleman knows that the greatest accomplishments he attains will come through the facts, thoughts and insights he has accumulated by the conversations he has, the books he reads, the things he studies and all the tidbits of information he picks up along the way.

As we have mentioned, the gentleman throughout history has been associated with education and knowledge. From the gentleman scholars of Greece and Roman, and onto the Renaissance and beyond, the gentleman always has a dazzling fact at his fingertips.

The pursuit of knowledge is a lifelong journey and an exciting one and once on the path, it is an immensely fulfilling and rewarding one.

A Gentleman's Hint:

For at least 30 minutes each day read a non-fiction book or magazine.

---

4. Masculinity

We believe in the **Gentle – Man,** the man who is firstly male and possessing male energy, then layering it with the aspects of gentleness and ease. The Gentleman sits on the spectrum between the Metro-Sexual and the Alpha Male.

As history shows through the ages, the gentleman skill sets always included physical and/or martial prowess. Nowadays the likelihood of being involved in combat on a daily basis (outside of the professional realms) is unlikely, but the ability to defend yourself, or those around you, gives you confidence, physical health and a martial skill, which may come in handy one day.

One of our favourite Martial Arts is Bartitsu. As James Marwood, Bartitsu Master, says, 'This martial art is the precursor to Bruce Lee's Jeet Kune Do and one of the earliest modern mixed martial arts.' Invented by a British Gentleman, Edgar Barton-Wright, Bartitsu found fame in the pages of Sherlock Holmes. It was invented for the mean streets of Victorian and Edwardian London but could fit into the streets of any modern day metropolis.

A Gentleman's Hint:

Find a sport/martial art/physical activity that you like and practice it at least once a week. Not only will it develop your masculinity but is good for your health as well.

Second Level – The External

External Values are the visible ones, the ones we display every day. These are the actions that show that you are a gentleman on the inside by displaying them to the world on the outside.

1. Style

Fashion fades, only style remains the same.

Coco Chanel

Though this is discussed in much more detail in the Stylish Gentleman chapter, the essence of style is to have elegance, a classical appearance that defines time. It is said that fashion is now and style is timeless.

It is not about being a carbon copy gentleman. It is about embracing the rules of appearance and taste and knowing what works for you and then embellishing with your personality. It is thinking about the impression you make and respecting your surroundings.

A Gentleman's Hint:

Dress each day as if you might meet someone who could change your life.

---

2. Chivalry

The motto of chivalry is also the motto of wisdom; to serve all, but love only one.

Honore de Balzac

Chilvary is defined as behaving courteously, especially towards women. To some it is a value that seems outdated and old fashioned, but is courteous behaviour a bad thing? Not in our book. We believe that the respect and courtesy a gentleman shows someone, female or not, is an exceptional thing. The modern gentleman shows chivalry to all.

It has become linked, wrongly, to a sense of superiority and misogyny on the part of men. Let's change it back to its true meaning of esteem.

Chivalry is courteous behaviour that goes that step beyond the Common Manners (See Below). These actions, such as holding a door open, offering your seat, rising to greet someone who enters the room and walking on the road-side of the pavement, show regard and appreciation for those people; Male or Female.

We have forgotten that the core of chivalry was about respecting people, especially ladies, and by these actions showing respect and humility to help others.

A Gentleman's Hint:

Do the little things: give up your seat, hold open the door and walk on the roadside of the pavement. See what happens.

---

3. Charm

> " You know what charm is: a way of getting the answer 'yes' without having asked any clear question."

Albert Camus

If a gentleman is charming, he can quickly overcome such problems as lack of funds, unfortunate looks and many other problems in his life, and this value alone can and will help him achieve many, many things.

What is being charming? Its definition and etymology all hint to a magical ability, a power to influence or delight. In essence it is the ability to make other people feel at ease and comfortable around you.

At its core it is about making the other person more important in the interaction than yourself, by learning about them and engaging with them on a personal level.

There are a number of skills and techniques about building exceptionally quick rapport with people, such as matching body language and speech patterns, these can be taught easily.

It does help if you can be witty, and have a joke or a self-deprecating anecdote to tell, but not all of us are stand-up comedians.

Be humble and self-effacing, which nicely moves us onto our next value.

A Gentleman's Hint:

Listen – all great communication is about listening first. Find out about them and then discuss what is important to them.

---

4. Humility

" Humility is not thinking less of yourself, it is thinking of yourself less."

C. S. Lewis

There are those that talk the talk and those that walk the walk and then there is the gentleman who walks on by without letting you know he was even there.

Humility is an interesting value, at its core is the ability to, as the Rudyard Kipling poem 'If' mentions, treat both triumph and disaster the same.

The gentleman is grateful for his successes and happiness and is aware that it can change in the blink of an eye. If that is in one's heart, then one can have humility.

A Gentleman's Hint:

If someone says or does something that annoys you or upsets you, place a wry smile on your face and think that they must be in a worse place than you to behave in that way.

Third Level – The Greater Good

The third level of values, are those that impact the world at large. Whether that is in a small way by just changing one situation or across the globe changing many lives.

1. Courage

> " Courage is resistance to fear, mastery of fear, not absence of fear."

Mark Twain

The highest military honour in the United Kingdom is that of the Victoria Cross. It is awarded to those who show courage under fire. Receivers of the honour have many great tales, but if you speak to them of the actions that won them the honour, they do not think of themselves as courageous.

Courage is about ability to face difficulty, danger or pain without succumbing to fear. To stand up for those who cannot, to believe in the greater good.

The philosophy of the gentleman throughout his history is one based on the core principle of courage. Dating as far back as the Code of Chivalry, a true Knight showed he could protect the weak and fight evil.

Courage does not need the grand gesture, it can be as simple as giving someone a shoulder to lean on, when you would rather not.

A Gentleman's Hint:

Start small. Stand up for your personal convictions. If you believe in something do not be afraid to defend it.

---

2. Honour

A man of honour should never forget what he is because he sees what others are.

Baltasar Gracian

Honour is that concept that falls into the mists of history and does not seem to raise its head in the modern world so much.

What is honour for the modern gentleman? Dr Johnson in his dictionary defined it as 'nobility of soul, magnanimity and a scorn of meanness.' It is bound up in reputation and the code of behaviour that defines that reputation.

Being that gentleman is about adhering to one's own code of honour based on the values that one holds true, such as those in here and those within one's cultural and social boundaries.

Honour is totally bound up in the actions that you take and the principles for which you stand, make them worthy of yourself, the gentlemen around you, and the world at Large.

A Gentleman's Hint:
Your Word is your bond – Never make a promise that you cannot keep. Again, start small. Keep your word, whether that be delivering a deadline, document or letter.

3. Loyalty

Within the hearts men, loyalty and consideration are esteemed greater than success.

Bryant H McGill

The Samurai in ancient Japan, would be so driven by loyalty to their master that if he failed him, disgraced him, or even lost him in battle, he would be expected to commit ritual suicide, in a show of loyalty.

This is extreme for the modern world, though we have once again left loyalty behind for speed of progress.

We are not saying that you need to work in a company for the next forty years or cling on as a marriage falls apart. We are saying that relationships, places and people need your effort and help to make them work and grow, and that takes some loyalty.

Let's put it into a modern context. Think about a Start Up business and a team of people that have come together to build a business. They have formed a bond, a code and group sense of loyalty to accomplish their goal of success. They might hit bumps along the road and have difficulties but their loyalty to each other and the course will see them through.

> **A Gentleman's Hint:**
> Show people you care for them and have them at heart. Do something with them in the next couple of days.

4. Compassion

> " *The purpose of human life is to serve, and to show compassion and the will to help others.* "

Albert Schweitzer

The deepest need of all humans on an emotional level is to be loved. This can be most easily demonstrated by a show of compassion.

Compassion for one's fellow man is to show that you can empathise with another's plight and, where we can, do something about it. It is at the core of most religious and ethical philosophies across the world.

This belief in the ability to empathise and then do something about it, with word or action is the thing that makes you a true gentleman.

> **A Gentleman's Hint:**
> Do at least one of these actions in the next couple of weeks: Next time you see a homeless person out on the street, offer to purchase them some food, whether it be hot or cold. Ask them what they would like. Or find a place to volunteer, either at a hospice or an old people's home or even an animal shelter.

We have summarised these values into a little Manifesto, which you can find at the end of the book or on our websites.

The Commons

The commons are anything but common. They are not exactly a value, but more of a skill that epitomizes some if not all the values.

Common Manners

The "Pleases & Thank Yous" that we need to use at all times. These are the little things that you use everyday such as excusing yourself if you sneeze (and use a handkerchief or tissue), letting people off the train first. These are the social glue, which helps society to function.

The Key List of 'Magic Words' - remember them well and use them frequently.

Please

Thank You

You are welcome

Excuse Me

I'm Sorry

Common Courtesies

It is the small things that matter most and it is the same with the common courtesies. Courtesies differ from the manners in that they require more positive action. They go beyond the general everyday of manners.

They include things such as writing 'Thank You' notes; going to someone's house with a gift; your behaviour on public transport and a variety of other little actions.

Common Decency

It is more common to be indecent that decent in today's world. Nowadays, we are shocked by good behaviour rather than appalled by the bad.

A gentleman should behave, dress and speak with a sense of decorum and with the thought that his sainted grandmother is watching him at all times.

Warren Buffet, one of the world's richest men, said always behave as if you appeared on the front pages of the newspaper and your life depended on your reputation.

Common Sense

For many years the department store Nordstrom, in the USA, gave each new employee a small grey card with just seventy-five words describing a single rule.

Nordstrom Rules: Rule #1: Use your best judgment in all situations. There will be no additional rules.

This was the ultimate use of common sense. It has now changed to add to the pile of regulations and expectations, but this core principle has served the company exceptionally well.

In Hagakure, a book on the way of being a samurai, the author writes that when the samurai is making a decision he should be still in thought for seven breaths, for during these seven breaths a clear decision can be made.

The core of the Gentleman is to live all of the values listed above. If you take these to heart and live them as best you can everyday, then everyday the journey will get easier and without realising it you will Become the Perfect Gentleman.

THE STYLISH GENTLEMAN

" Menswear is about subtlety. It's about good style and good taste."

Alexander McQueen

Introduction

The Perfectly Stylish Gentleman should always be correctly dressed for the occasion; he should take care of his appearance but appear 'effortlessly stylish'. But to achieve this takes work and consistent attention to detail. It is a level of style to which we should all aspire, and for many of us it is a marathon rather than a sprint.

The amount of money you have should not restrict your ability to be a Stylish Gentleman. In this chapter we will tell you how we believe you can be stylish whether your budget takes you to online retailers, chain stores, vintage and charity shops or Savile Row.

Why is it important to be Stylish?

Most importantly your style will reflect your personality. As the saying goes "there is never a second chance to make a first impression", and in many cases the way you dress and are groomed will be a big part of the impression you make on people.

Building a Wardrobe

In this chapter our aim is to show you how to start building your wardrobe, outlining the key fourteen items that you will need, which can be mixed for work, formal and casual occasions.

These fourteen items will form the foundation of your wardrobe. Once you have them right, you can start to consider how to further expand your wardrobe and add the stylish flourishes, which will set you apart.

We have built this wardrobe so that it can be purchased at any budget. In fact we have found all the items for as little as £500 ($750). For more up to date prices go to our website.

The Essential 14 items you need for a basic wardrobe

1. *One Navy (or Black) suit*

2. *One dark Jacket*

3. *Two formal shirts (white)*

4. *Two formal shirts (blue)*

5. *One pair of formal shoes (black)*

6. *One pair of formal shoes (brown)*

7. *One pair of casual trousers (dark blue or similar)*

8. *Two t-shirts (white)*

9. *One v-neck jumper (tan or light)*

10. *One v-neck jumper (blue or darker)*

11. *One reversible belt (brown/black)*

> ### A Gentleman's Hints:
>
> For the purpose of this guide we have excluded from this list items such as underwear, socks, ties and pocket-handkerchiefs. We assume that these items can be taken care of by the gentleman himself.

1. The Suit

Many people today consider wearing a suit to be 'dressing up'. But wearing a suit will clearly define you and mark you out as a gentleman.

The ideal suit is elegant and your basic suits should be plain colours, ideally dark blue and/or black. As you grow your wardrobe you can start to add suits, but think carefully about where you will wear a suit. Dark colours are sober for serious work meetings and can be brightened and lifted with a colourful tie and pocket square; in the right circumstances.

So how to decide which suit to buy? There is a huge market with an enormous price range. It is possible to pay anywhere between £90 and £4,000 for a suit. With a gap that large it is critical that you know what you are doing when you set out to make your purchase.

So here is the Perfect Gentleman's step-by-step guide to buying a suit:

Step 1 - Budget

First check your budget and decide how much you have to spend. Our rough guide would be:

Off the Peg Suits (anywhere between £90 and £500+)

This is how the majority of the world buys their suits. There is a huge range of choices available from the £90 polyester suit from an online retailer to pure new wool, wool or mohair, available from some of the leading high street chains.

When you go to buy a suit from a chain store always make sure that you are wearing a shirt and tie and the shoes you will be wearing with the suit. This will allow you to get the 'full effect' when you try on the trousers and jacket.

Sizing

When you buy suits from a large national chain you will usually find that the jackets will be available in 2" increments of chest size with short, regular and long arms.

The jacket length is a matter of choice, but you should aim to select a jacket in which, with your arms hanging loosely by your sides, your fingers should curl up naturally under the bottom of the jacket.

To ensure that you select the right sleeve length, aim to have about 1" of shirt cuff showing when your arms are hanging by your sides.

Trousers will usually be available in a variety of waist and leg sizes. In this way you can find the store that suits you and your budget. It also makes buying your second suit very quick as you can quickly find your size or even order on-line from the same store with confidence that the suit will fit.

One pair of trousers or two?

Individual elements of the suit are usually priced separately. You will notice that the jacket is by far the most expensive element. If you are buying a suit, which you will use on a daily basis for work, it is worth considering buying two pairs of trousers. Long hours sitting at a desk or in a car can mean that trousers wear more quickly than the jacket, which can spend a lot of the day on a hanger. This means that if/when the trousers are no longer serviceable you can find yourself with an expensive jacket left over. It is also worth considering whether you wish to add a waistcoat to the suit.

Alterations

If you buy a good quality 'off the peg' suit and the fit is not quite right, it may be worth enlisting the help of an 'alteration tailor'. There are many of these if you look around and they will be able to take a standard suit and make subtle alterations to personalise the suit for you.

Made to Measure Suits (anywhere between £800 and £3,000)

A made to measure suit would normally be based on an existing design that is mass-produced in a factory where stitching is done by machine. You will have a level of customisation in the design process. This may consist of picking different cloths, lapels, pockets, buttons, cuffs and much more. The biggest difference in the process is the person taking your measurements, they will probably not be a tailor used to taking a multitude of measurements. It is also very rare that you will have a full canvas suit. Most made to measure suits will come back with a half canvas that will stop just beneath the chest with the area below that fuse to give the fronts stiffness.

Bespoke Suits (between £2,500 and £4,000)

A tailor, with whom you personally consult, makes the bespoke suit. They take dozens of body measurements and create a unique suit for your body, which will be hand cut and entirely stitched from your chosen materials, using an 'in house' workshop. This process requires at least one basic fitting and if need be a second advanced fitting. The suit will normally have a full floating canvas (the reinforcement which keeps the suit's shape) and not use any fuse or glue in the construction. The bespoke tailor will be able to offer you a near unlimited number of cloth choices and weights to cater for your lifestyle and needs.

Step 2 - Visiting your Tailor (Bespoke and made to measure suits)

Always dress well when you visit your tailor, it shows respect for him and will motivate him when he sees that you care about your clothes. Ideally wear a suit, which you like (cut, style etc.). It will give him useful hints for the suit he is going to make for you. Make sure you are wearing a shirt with sleeve lengths that you prefer.

In terms of payment, most tailors will expect to be paid a deposit of half the final cost of the suit when the first measurements are taken to cover production costs. From this point you should anticipate that your final suit will be delivered in around six weeks.

Step 3 – Choosing your fabric

The type of fabric you select can make a huge difference to the cost of the final suit, so choose carefully. If this is your first suit we suggest you select a wool fabric with a grade of 100s or 110 and about 9/10 ounces, an ideal medium weight and one you can wear all year round.

The grade indicates how fine the cloth is. Super 120/130 cloths are often recommended but will be expensive. Similarly, lightweight cloths should be avoided for a first suit as they can damage easily and will not hold their shape well.

Choosing the colour of the fabric is a highly personal matter but we suggest that for your first suits a dark blue or black is ideal as these are suitable for many occasions.

As you extend your wardrobe of suits you can get more adventurous with colours, stripes and also consider lighter weight suits for summer and heavier fabric or tweeds for the colder months.

Step 4 – Measurements

At this point your tailor will take all the measurements required to make a suit for your particular 'body shape' to ensure that your suit fits you like a glove.

He will want to know how you would like the suit to fall on your shoulders, where you like to wear your trousers (i.e. waist or hips) and to see how you like your trouser legs to fall on your shoes.

If you have decided to have a 'made to measure' suit your tailor may use 'shell fittings' instead of taking measurements. This will require you to try on standard garments until the nearest size fit is found, at which point the sales staff will record what changes need to be made to this pattern size to make it a better fit.

Step 5 - Selecting the Style

Jacket/Coat

At this point you need to make some decisions. One, two or three buttons? Single or double breasted? One vent or two? If this is your first suit look at some pictures in magazines or on the web, find a style you like. Or pop into a large chain store branch and try on a few jackets by way of 'research'. Just make sure you are properly dressed (i.e. shirt and tie) as it is impossible to try out a jacket if you are wearing a t-shirt.

The choice of jacket will depend on your body shape and the current styles at the time of your purchase. The two button single-breasted suit is the safest look on most men; a short man is often suited to a one-button suit. You can discuss your options with your tailor, as he has probably seen every suit style and will be able to make a recommendation.As with off the peg suits, the jacket length is a matter of personal preference, however as a rule, with your arms hanging loosely by your sides, your fingers should curl up naturally under the bottom of the jacket. Sleeve length when relaxed should show three-eighths of an inch of shirt at the cuffs.

The rear vents on a jacket allow comfort and movement; you can have one, two or no rear vents. But no vents is really only suited to dinner jackets.

Each cuff should have four buttons. As with all the visible buttons on the suit, they must be made of real horn, with a bespoke suit real horn buttons will be used automatically, on made to measure suits it will probably be imitation horn or plastic. The cuff buttonholes should be working; some tailors like to make two real buttonholes and two sham ones on each cuff, to facilitate future alteration of the sleeve length. This can spoil the appearance.

While wearing working cuff buttons it is not proper, indeed, it is considered the height of vulgarity, to leave any of them open in public.

Lapel buttonhole

The left lapel of a single-breasted jacket should have a buttonhole for the wearing of a flower, with a loop on the underside of the lapel to secure the flower stem. A double-breasted jacket (and a single-breasted jacket with peak lapels) might additionly have a buttonhole in the right lapel – but this is a matter of individual taste. Some argue that this second buttonhole adds an appearance of balance; others believe it to be over-fussy.

Trouser

Trousers do not hang properly without the assistance of braces. We recommend that provision for braces should therefore be made.

Lining

An inner silk lining to the front of the trousers, down to about the level of the knee, will prevent any unpleasant rubbing of the woolen cloth on the skin of your leg.

Pockets

Front pockets on flat front trouser look modern but are impractical to use, side pockets are the best all round choice. It is a temptation to carry items in the rear hip pockets, but this can ruin the line of the jacket and is best avoided.

Pleats

Again flat front trousers give the cleanest and most modern look, but for comfort one or two front pleats on either side of the front should be stipulated. They can point outwards or inwards, according to taste.

A zip is fine on a made to measure suit but a bespoke suit should have a button fly.

Step 6: Personalise it

The beauty of a tailored suit is that you can add personal touches to make your suit look genuine and unique. Whether it is specific types of buttons, linings, embroidery, or indeed pockets, just ask the tailor. A made to measure service will offer fewer options.

Step 7: First fitting

Within weeks you should expect your first fitting if you have chosen the bespoke route. This will be your final chance to make changes to the lapel width, button position, number of pockets and most of the other final details can still be changed before completion of the suit. If you have chosen made to measure you should expect your finished suit at this point and should skip to Step 8.

Step 8: Finished Suit

At this stage, you will need to look over every detail. Do not hesitate to ask for a little adjustment; you are paying for the suit and should make sure that everything fits to your liking. The tailor will ask you to try on the suit so that he personally check every angle to make sure your suit is perfect.

At this stage, it is also time to pay the tailor's final bill, and as you write out the cheque be sure to reflect that you are not just buying an item of clothing but making an investment in a hand- made suit, which if you treat it with respect, will last you for many wonderful years.

2. One dark Jacket

Pick the right jacket and it will be ideal for smart and casual occasions. Nowadays blazers are a bit 'passé' unless you want to make a fashion statement, so we recommend a classic dark blue jacket instead.

We suggest that you choose this particular item with great care and consider investing in a good quality jacket, as its flexibility is likely to make it a major 'work horse' of your wardrobe.

A good dark jacket opens up a world of possibilities in both formal and casual situations. It can be worn with dark or light trousers, shirt and tie for formal occasions, or with chinos or jeans and an open neck shirt or t-shirt for casual occasions.

3. Two formal shirts (white)

Good quality white shirts work in any circumstances. They are ideal for work and cool for casual wear with or without a tie. Find a good maker or chain store brand that you like. Key items to consider are the collar style (button down, cut back, etc.) and the cuffs (single/double button, or cufflinks). In some cases it is possible to get shirts which have a single button, but which can also be used with cufflinks when you want to push the sartorial boat out.

4. Two formal shirts (blue)

As with the formal white shirts consider the style carefully, but a blue shirt is probably more likely to be used in both formal and informal situations so this should be considered when selecting the style.

5. One pair of formal shoes (black)

Shoes are one of the key parts of your wardrobe and the quality of your shoes and the way they are kept will mark you out. As your first pair of black shoes we recommend a solid pair of Oxfords. Consider carefully how much to invest in them. A good, solid pair of leather soled shoes can be purchased for a little over £100 and if they are good quality shoes they can be re-soled and will last you many years. Consider having the heels quarter tipped by your cobbler to extend the life of the heels.

6. One pair of formal shoes (brown)

Think hard about the brown shoes because they are the most likely to be worn with casual clothes and jeans. A really classic pair of good brown brogues works well with a blue suit and jeans. As always with shoes, think of them as an investment. Good, leather soled shoes combined with a good cobbler can keep your shoes running and serviceable for 15 or 20 years depending on how often and hard you wear them. In the long run this will make them far cheaper and more characterful than a cheap throw away pair of shoes.

7. One Pair of casual trousers (dark blue)

Dark blue trousers are ideal for casual wear and work well with black or brown shoes and in a variety of casual circumstances. When selecting them choose a medium weight fabric that is suitable all year round.

8. Two t-shirts (white)

White T-shirts are incredibly versatile. Worn with casual trousers, under a blue shirt with an open neck is a great casual look, as is a white t-shirt under a v neck jumper. They will also provide that extra layer worn under a business shirt and suit on a cold day.

9. One v neck jumper (tan)

We have suggested v neck jumpers for their flexibility. They can be worn with a shirt (and/or tie) or a t-shirt. They look good on their own or under a jacket on a cooler day. A light tan jumper works well with either a blue or white shirt.

10. One v neck jumper (blue)

Another of the workhorses of the wardrobe, a blue v neck jumper is perfect in very many circumstances and could even be worn under a suit on a cold day in all but the most formal occasions.

11. One reversible belt (brown/black)

There is a key reason that we specify a double-sided belt. Matching colours is critical and you must always match the colour of your belt and your shoes. You may have to hunt around a little for a double-sided belt and you may consider buying two belts, but ensuring you are matching is critical.

There is an old adage 'never brown in town', but today this is really considered passé, brown shoes are perfectly acceptable.

12. The Extra Embellishments

a. Ties

In most business situations it is still required that you wear a tie. For the Perfect Gentleman wearing a tie will not only complete your stylish look but it also shows that, in an age when many people will wear a suit with an open necked shirt, you have made the effort to dress properly.

Learn to tie your tie properly; there are a huge variety of knots, but if you know how to do a standard Windsor knot you will not go far wrong. You will need to periodically check that your tie is snug and tight. There is nothing worse than a loose tie where the top button is visible. Always keep your top shirt button done up when you are wearing a tie. Never slacken your tie off, either wear a tie properly or take it off all together.

b. Pocket square

A beautiful silk pocket square may only cost a few pounds but it adds a distinctive air of colour and individuality to a dark suit.

There is a multitude of ways to wear a pocket square whether it is flamboyant with the corners of the square all showing or restrained with just a little folded colour showing above the line of the breast pocket. Pick a style to suit the occasion. The fact that you took the trouble will mark you out as a gentleman.

c. Cravat

At the Perfect Gentleman we believe there should be no such thing as 'Dress down Friday'. We believe that a gentleman should dress down to the point of wearing a cravat on a Friday. They look very stylish with an open necked shirt and they will mark you out among your colleagues at the end of the week.

d. Socks

Socks are another way of marking you out as an individual in a world of greys and dark blues. A stunning pair of colourful socks peeping out from beneath a sober suit can mark you out as an individual in a homogenized and standardised world.

Taking Care of Your Wardrobe

Once you have carefully selected the fourteen items for your wardrobe the key point is to ensure that everything is cared for, clean and well looked after. You must always look smart and maximize the life of your clothes and shoes.

General rules

- *Find a good dry cleaner that you can trust.* Your beautiful suit, jackets and trousers will, in most cases specify 'dry clean only'. To find a good dry cleaner, check with your friends (male and female), and possibly put in an old suit or jacket to test the service before you trust them with your brand new suit.

- *Protect your wardrobe against moths.* There is nothing worse than investing in a good wool suit or a beautiful cashmere jumper only to take it out of the wardrobe and find small holes caused by moths. It is no longer necessary to use foul smelling mothballs. Many stores stock pine balls, which will keep your clothes safe. If you are putting something away for a longer period consider storing it in a sealable plastic hanger bag.

- *Learn how to use a washing machine.* Take responsibility for keeping your clothes clean and smart, and take the time to understand the workings of your washing machine. Washing your own clothes means you will only have yourself to blame if your best white shirt is turned pink by a rogue red sock.

- *Learn how to iron a shirt and to press your trousers.* If your mother never taught you how to iron your shirts, it is about time you learnt. It is not difficult, and with a couple of hours practice you will be turning out perfectly pressed shirts.

- *Buttons.* When you buy a new suit or shirt you will usually find a small plastic bag of buttons in one of the pockets, or a spare button sown inside a shirt. We advise you to store these in one safe place so that you can find the right button if/when you lose one.

Suits and Jackets

- Get proper heavy wooden hangers that will keep the jacket shape. Always hang the trousers and check carefully that the creases are lined up every time you hang them.

- When your suits and jackets come back from the dry cleaners be sure to take them off the wire hangers. This will ensure your jackets stay in shape and will avoid those unsightly creases across the knees of your trousers.

- Think very carefully before you put anything in the pockets of your suit. Nothing looks worse than baggy pockets.

- Always unbutton your jacket before you sit down to avoid pulling at the buttons.

- Keep your jacket buttoned when standing

- Button rules

- Two button suits, both buttons done up

- Three buttons – bottom button undone

- Waistcoat – bottom button undone (always)

Trousers

- If you work in an office your trousers will take a lot of punishment. To ensure they are kept smart, and to avoid nasty creasing behind the knees, they should be sponged over lightly and pressed regularly.

- These days we tend to carry large smart phones, wallets and keys in our trouser pockets, which will spoil the line of your suit. Consider putting your phone and keys in your briefcase/bag and always ensure your wallet is cleared of old receipts regularly to keep it slim and minimize space in your pocket.

Shirts and T shirts

- Consider adding a small amount of starch when washing your shirts or use a spray starch on your shirtfronts, cuffs and collars just before ironing. This will give your shirt an additional crisp sharpness.

- Men love to keep a favourite shirt, but there comes a time when it needs to be consigned to cleaning the car or dumped.

- Periodically you will lose a button, so make sure you have a needle and thread handy (you will need the right colour threads for shirts) and then get someone who knows to show you how it is done.

Shoes

- Investing in good shoes and taking care of them should ensure that they last you for many years.

- Invest in a proper polish (we love the Kiwi Parade polish) and a pair of good brushes. Learn how to clean your shoes properly and clean them regularly. First, wipe your shoes down with a lightly damped cloth, then apply the polish generously leaving the polish to 'soak in' to each shoe for a short while. Then buff the polish into a shine with the second brush and finish them off with a duster to get a perfect shine. If you have good leather shoes with a solid toe-cap, follow the full instructions on Kiwi Parade polish to get that amazing Guardsman's mirror like finish.

- Remember that walking on a new pair of leather soles can be like walking on sheet ice on some surfaces, so consider scoring the leather lightly in a crisscross pattern to give you some 'grip'

- If you have bought leather soled shoes be sure to' wear them in' in dry conditions before you wear them out in the wet to allow the soles to get a 'seal'.

- If you have really good shoes, consider cedar shoe trees to keep the shape and to dry out any perspiration in the warmer months.

Jumpers

- Always put your jumpers away carefully. Either hang them on a wooden hanger or fold them carefully.

- Look at the washing and drying instructions carefully and ensure that your washing machine has the correct low temperature setting for fine woollen garments. Many a great sweater has been reduced to a size fit only for Action Man by washing at too high a temperature.

- If you have a very fine jumper consider hand washing it only, and once it has been washed and rinsed allow it to dry lying flat on an old towel to ensure it retains its shape.

Other items

- Always have a proper place to hang your ties to avoid them getting creased

- When a tie has come to the end of its 'natural life' throw it out. Our suggestion would be to always buy ties in the sales. Get three or four and hold a couple back opening a new one for special meetings or dates.

These are the very basics of being stylish, and indeed our very next book, Becoming the Stylish Gentleman, will take you through a guided tour of Men's Style and building out your wardrobe in stages. If you cannot wait that long, seek solace in our magazine www.codeofthegentleman.com for more articles and inspiration.

THE GROOMED GENTLEMAN

" *You are your greatest asset. Put your time, effort and money into training, grooming, and encouraging your greatest asset.* "

Tom Hopkins

Introduction

A recent article in the Sunday Times (UK) revealed that the average British male spends £1,786 per year on grooming products. While 50% of that figure is made up of 'body sprays' and fragrances, over 11% is skin care, with shaving preparations at 9%.

Now while this may not be a surprise, what is amazing is male spending lags only slightly behind and is rapidly catching the British woman, who spends an average of £2,462 per year on cosmetics.

What is clear is that men are focusing much more on how they look and how they groom themselves. The Groomed Gentleman chapter will guide you through all aspects of grooming and provide an introduction to the basic grooming necessities that no Gentleman should be without.

So why is grooming so important to a gentleman?

It shows you care about yourself. Unfortunately it is true that first impressions last and the way people first see you will govern the way they deal with you. Being well groomed is one of the elements, together with the way you dress, which will create a positive impression.

You will look more healthy, and healthy looking skin and hair lifts your appearance and will give you a boost when you look in the mirror, improving your self confidence and the way others see you.

Achieving the look of 'The Perfectly Groomed Gentleman' does not happen by accident. It takes work, practice and effort. You will need to experiment, discover things about your skin and your hair. Find out what works best for you and create a grooming regime that works for you.

A Grooming Regime?

The Perfectly Groomed Gentleman does not achieve good skin, good hair and an overall good look by a quick wash and brush up on a Saturday night or just before an important meeting or date. What is required is a regular grooming regime, which pays attention to all aspects of grooming. While this may be difficult at the start, once established it will become second nature. It is important to have a regular regime not just that one night a week.

Learn & practice

To create a regime and to find the right products for shaving, skin care and for washing and styling your hair you need to be open to new products and techniques of grooming. Sticking to your existing ways and products may not be enough. Be open to new ideas and take time to try new things and practice new techniques.

Explore: Try products when you have time

The ideal time to try something new is on a quiet weeknight or on a Sunday morning when you have time to experiment. It is also a good idea to try something new when you do not have an important date or meeting just in case you are allergic to something or if over enthusiastic washing or cleaning of your skin leaves it red or blotchy.

Practice, develop and hone your regime

Like anything worthwhile the key to getting your grooming regime right is practicing and repeating it, finding little improvements and working those in to your daily grooming and gradually refining it.

You may well find that a deep clean of your facial skin may only be necessary once or twice a week. Shaving properly, that means a full wet shave, every day, with possibly a rest on Sunday if you do not have anything to dress up for, will toughen your skin up and mean that you have fewer cuts and spots caused by ingrowing hairs.

Work your favourite bits into your regular regime

We all have particular areas of grooming that we enjoy and some that are more of a chore. If you have a regularly laid out regime try to do some of the chores first and leave yourself a couple of the more pleasurable items to the end.

Go to an expert

The key point in creating and maintaining the perfect grooming regime and gaining a Perfectly Groomed look is to find an expert who you respect and consult them on your regime, but also be prepared to go back to them if there are areas which require improving or particular focus.

The Perfect Gentleman works with a number of such experts and through the Weekly Code of the Gentleman newsletter, and on our website, we will introduce you to new grooming techniques, as well as friends and partners who will be able to help you refine your grooming regime.

A Gentleman's Hints:

- Find experts you like and trust and who you can go to with issues

- Read and digest items in the press and online, indeed on our website. Try out suggestions and be open to new ideas

---

Shaving

For most men shaving is a daily regime and yet it is something that few have been taught, in fact some statistics say as many as 95% have never been taught. A proper daily shaving regime will leave your skin in better condition and can result in far fewer spots and blemishes caused by ingrowing hairs.

Is shaving something you can be taught?

At a recent Perfect Gentleman Training event we took the opportunity to ask the assembled gentlemen how they learned to shave. The vast majority had either taught themselves to shave or at best had been given a disposable razor and an aerosol of shaving foam by their Dad and pointed in the direction of a mirror.

How much training have you had?

From our investigations we believe that most men are self-taught and have had no formal training. This usually means that there are huge improvements that can be made in your shaving regime, in the quality and therefore the longevity of each shave and ultimately in the quality of your skin after shaving.

Have a proper regime

Develop a proper shaving regime, find products and 'tools' that suit you and your skin and learn how to use them for best effect. You may well find that the full regime can take too long on a work day, and is best left for on a Saturday evening. You may want to develop a shorter version if time is pressing on a day when you have an early start or if you have overslept.

A wet shave takes the same time as an electric shave

The wet shave is better for you; it leaves skin feeling cleaner. You may have started your shaving life using an electric razor and may only rarely have used a wet razor. Certainly if you have a light growth you may get away with an electric shave. Our experience is that however good an electric razor is there are areas of your face on which it is not possible to get a good result, we find areas get missed and your face is left feeling scrubbed and itchy.

On the other hand, using a wet razor leaves the skin feeling fresh and clean and the results, in our experience, are always better. We would also maintain that if you shave regularly you can achieve a great result with a wet shave in the same time as it takes to have an electric shave.

What is a proper shave?

Everyone will develop their own shaving regime but this is our recommendation, developed through taking a proper shaving lesson from the professionals at Geo Trumpers and our friends at the Refinery in London, developing the technique through experience and working with our partners to test and identify the right shaving products. It works for us and some members of the Perfect Gentlemen team have particularly heavy growth of beard.

1. Wash

The ideal preparation for a shave is a soak in a hot bath or a hot shower. The steam will start to warm and clean the skin and soften the bristles. If you are shaving on a morning you are not showering make sure to wash your face as thoroughly as possible in water that is as hot as possible using a little soap. In a proper barber they will use a hot towel to warm the skin and soften the bristles. At home, when there is time, the same effect can be achieved by using a flannel soaked in hot water (as hot as you can bear). Place the hot flannel over your face for a minute or two. Repeat this process once or twice for the best results.

2. Prepare the Skin

Preparing the skin is a key stage and one that is very often missed when shaving at home. It will make a huge difference to the final smoothness of your shave. Ultimately this is a matter of preference, but having tried a number of different lotions and potions we find the best results are achieved using shaving oil. A small amount squeezed into the palm of one hand and then massaged gently into clean, warmed chin and cheeks, creates the perfect base for the next stage.

3. Lather

It is quick, easy and, the adverts would have you believe, better, to use an aerosol soap product to achieve a lather. We have consistently found that the little extra time taken to use a proper shaving brush and shaving cream to work up a thick smooth lather and apply it to your face gives a far better result.

Using a good quality shaving brush also has the added advantage, if done fairly vigorously, of lifting up the hairs and stimulating the skin before shaving.

While we do not have any empirical data to quote here, we are certain that using a small amount of good quality shaving cream each day is far more economical than using an aerosol. In our experience that it is only necessary to buy a new tub of cream every 12 – 16 months, rather than getting through four or five cans of aerosol shaving foam a year.

The other advantage is that it is possible to find more natural shaving creams without the nasty, skin-drying chemicals used in many of the popular commercial brands.

4. Razor

If you treat yourself to a barber's wet shave they will almost certainly use a cutthroat razor. Nowadays cutthroats have more generally been replaced with safety razors with an increasing number of blades. It is our experience that providing you follow this or a similar regime, and you fairly regularly change your blade, you can achieve a result every bit as 'baby bottom' smooth using a safety razor as your skilled barber will achieve with his cutthroat.

The key point is to warm the blades of the razor in hot water before you start to shave and frequently wash off the lather either under a tap or in a basin to keep the blades clean.

When you have a professional Barber's shave they may well go over your chin a second time, this is because they will shave each area twice, once in each direction. As you get to know your own face you will discover which direction gives the best results and this may well vary for different parts of your face. While you may want to go over certain areas a second time for a perfect shave, in most cases it is not necessary to go over the whole face twice.

The point at which you change to a new blade is a personal choice. Many of the modern multi blade razors will have a moisture gel band, or some such wonderful addition, to ease the passing of the razor. Often this runs out long before the blades become dull or blunted and with correct preparation and lather they are not required. We would advise you to change to a new blade when you feel the old blade starting to pull a little. If you have a heavy growth of beard this will be more frequently than you if you have a light growth. If you have a major event like a wedding or a big interview always use a new blade to get the very best effect.

5. Clean

When you are satisfied that you have achieved a good clean shave the next stage is to wash your face thoroughly in clean water. Empty the basin of soapy water and either run a clean bowl or run the tap.

Many shaving soaps will have a drying effect on the skin and so should be washed off. Patting the face with cool or cold water at the end of this stage is a good way to calm down the face and close down the pores, which will have been opened by the hot water.

6. Cuts

Cuts generally happen when shaving because you have small spots or blemishes on your skin. A good washing or skin cleaning regime (if you have particularly oily skin) will reduce the outbreak of spots and using a shaving oil will reduce the number of spots caused by ingrowing hairs by ensuring the razor works efficiently.

If you are susceptible to spots and cuts you may need to invest in s styptic pencil or an alum block, which will help close up small cuts and calm the skin after shaving.

7. Moisturise

After shaving it is extremely important to moisturise the skin. Find a product that suits you; one that does not irritate your skin, which can be difficult when your skin is freshly shaved and 'raw'. Ideally a good moisturiser should have some sun protection (SPF Factor) included and this applies all year round as the sun can have an aging effect on your skin at tall times of the year not just in the high summer.

How will I notice the difference?

When you have established a good shaving regime you will find that your skin feels cleaner and as your skin becomes used to regular shaving you will have fewer spots due to ingrowing hairs.

Skin Care

Once upon a time men used to deny using moisturiser, afraid of being called a 'metro-sexual'. Today grooming products for men are mainstream and men can freely admit to taking care of themselves.

Different types of skin?

You may be able to work out your skin type yourself or you may decide to consult a professional. Typically your skin will be either dry or oily/greasy, or possibly combination skin with some areas being greasy and some areas normal or dryer.

It should not be rocket science to work out which you have, although there will be different scales of dryness or greasiness to your skin and this can also be impacted by what you are doing or the conditions in which you live or work.

Also some skins that appear to be regular or quite dry, can become more greasy if you have a very vigorous cleaning regime which opens up your pores.

How should skin be cleaned?

Most men will wash their faces only when they get dirty and possibly when they are in the shower, although washing your face in the shower can lead to soap in your eyes so it is often something that is omitted.

Normal hand soap can be very drying to the skin so ideally use a non-soap face wash. These are commonly available and will gently clean the skin without drying and this is something that can be done every two or three days to keep the skin fresh and healthy.

In some areas it may be necessary to use a more abrasive skin cleaner or scrub to keep pores clean. Apply a small amount to a sponge or small pad and apply in a circular motion. This deeper cleaning should only be necessary every four to seven days according to how dirty your skin gets and the environment in which you live, work and travel every day.

If you have particularly oily skin, and this is very often the case for younger gentlemen, lack of cleaning of pores can lead to a build up which causes blackheads and spots. In this case there are daily skin cleaning lotions available, often spirit based, which should be applied with a clean cotton pad, again in a circular motion, to clean oily residue from pores and prevent a build up turning into something more serious.

How does my life/job affect my skin?

Where you work and the job you do is likely to have a major effect on your skin and how you treat it to make sure it stays healthy and looking good.

If you work outside you will need to consider the effects of cold weather, sun and wind, all of which will dry the skin and can lead to premature aging of the skin. Apply a healthy layer of moisturiser in the morning and at night, and ensure that you have some sun protection all year round. Make sure that in the summer it is particularly strong to avoid serious damage to your skin.

If you work in an air conditioned office or spend a lot of time in the car your skin is likely to be dried by air conditioning. Make sure that you rehydrate by drinking plenty of water and moisturise your skin regularly.

How should I care for my skin?

Caring for your skin, keeping it clean and protected from the elements and from your environment is critical. Healthy looking skin is not just a result of caring for it externally it is also helped by eating a good diet, exercising and maintaining a good regime of hydration.

Why is moisturising important?

Moisturising and protecting your skin from the harmful effects of the sun will help you maintain good looking, healthy skin as you grow older and taking account of your working environment is a key part of this.

Care for your skin, keep it clean, moisturise and protect it all year round and you will be rewarded with a healthy glow and youthful, wrinkle free looks as you grow older.

Hair

Head hair is one of the Gentleman's most visible aspects, and ensuring that it is well cut, styled and clean at all times will mark out the Perfect Gentleman.

Having your hair cut

It is possible to spend anywhere between £5 and £50+ ($7.50-$80+) on a haircut and if you venture into some of the salons of London's Mayfair and seek out a top stylist you could probably pay far more. However, once you are out on the street it is often very difficult to tell who spent what on their hair, so the key point is to find a barber or hairdresser who you trust and who cuts your hair the way you like and within your budget. Then make sure that you go to him regularly.

A hairdresser we know always says that if you look in the mirror and decide that you need a haircut then it is already too late! Set a regular gap between haircuts and stick to it. This is probably likely to be once every three to four weeks depending on the length of your hair.

How often should I wash my hair?

If you shower daily then it is highly likely that you will wash your hair daily. This can be too often, particularly if you use a strong shampoo. Try washing your hair less frequently to retain the natural oils in your hair and make it healthier.

Some hairdressers suggest rinsing your hair with water only in the shower to allow styling and only use shampoo when your hair is really dirty.

Is a conditioner important?

When washing your hair you should always add a conditioner after washing. It will greatly improve the quality and manageability of your hair. We would generally recommend that you use a separate conditioner. Combined shampoo and conditioners are not as effective.

What 'product' should I use on my hair?

There are a huge range of gels and other products available to aid the styling of your hair. Using these means that your hair will need to be washed more frequently in order to maintain your style. If it is possible to style your hair without adding anything you will be able to wash your hair less frequently and it will be in better condition.

What do I do if I need help with grey hair?

These days there is a huge range of products available to disguise or remove grey hair. The best thing is to take advice from a professional hairdresser or a professional grooming salon to avoid using something that is visible.

Beards and facial hair

With the popularity of 'Movember' and many fashionable people looking to the past for fashion cues, moustaches and beards are gaining in popularity. So, if you are joining the trend, it is important you keep yours in good trim.

Is stubble Gentlemanly?

Carefully controlled stubble can look great on a gentleman, the key is to define the edges so that your stubble is clearly a fashion statement rather than a sign that you have been too lazy to shave for a couple of days.

Clippers and shaping

A good adjustable electric beard trimmer will allow you to maintain the stubble at a consistent length if you go over it every three or four days.

Oiling and cleaning the beard

Washing and caring for a beard can be difficult. Our experience is that the less often you wash your beard the less of an issue itching will be. However, if you never wash your beard you will become very 'unpopular', so wash it as infrequently as possible and condition it with normal hair conditioner or beard oil.

Moustache care and wax

If you decide not to grow a 'full set' then growing a moustache may be the stylish answer and if you decide to grow a longer moustache then wax will be required to keep it styled and disciplined. Many good moustache waxes are available, so try a couple out to find your favourite. Our experience is that they are all of a similar strength and the amount of control they exert is a function of the amount applied.

A top moustache wax tip is to keep your wax on a radiator overnight to ensure that it is soft and malleable in the morning. If you need it during the day keep it in a hip pocket during the colder months.

Fragrances

The days of the room filling with overpowering aftershave are long gone. Today's advertisers would have you believe that you need a powerful body spray to guarantee success with women. The truth for the Perfect Gentleman is far more sparing and subtle.

How do I select a fragrance?

Selecting a fragrance is a highly personal choice and a Gentleman may well have more than one scent.

When selecting a scent, go to a large department store where there is plenty of choice or, if you are in London, go to one of the specialist perfumers in St James's or Mayfair.

The first test should be to sniff the top of the sample bottle to get an indication of the scent. When you find one you like, spray a good sample onto the inside of your wrist, then go and have a coffee and only when your skin has warmed the scent and any spirit has evaporated, should you smell it.

Never trust the paper sample strips you will see in the stores - always test a new scent on your skin and let it develop before you make a decision.

What fragrance is right for me?

This is a hugely personal decision, and if your other half has strong views you might want to involve her. As you are likely to be choosing a fragrance that you will use for many months, possibly years, make sure you take your time over the decision.

How should I use my fragrance?

Television adverts used to show man taking large handfuls of aftershave and slapping them onto freshly shaved cheeks. If you have ever done this you will know it is incredibly painful so apply moisturiser to your face and then add your fragrance to the pulse points such as wrists and the chest. As your body warms the scent will be projected.

One key point here is to decide what fragrance you are going to use and only use that one fragrance. Using a shower gel with a powerful smell, hair products with strong scents followed by a fragrance will just cause a jumble of clashing smells.

How much is the right amount?

Use a small amount of very good fragrance rather than a huge amount of cheap fragrance. Men's body sprays are very heavily advertised and smell extremely false and chemical. Buy a really good quality fragrance and use it sparingly.

Oral health

Bad oral health can cause bad breath and, if you are going to get close to someone in a business or a romantic situation, this can be very unpleasant, so pay particular attention to oral health.

Why is oral health important?

Oral health is important not only because regular brushing of your teeth and the daily use of dental floss will ensure your breath is pleasant, but it will also reduce the likelihood that you will require fillings and other highly expensive dental work.

What regime should a Gentleman have?

Hopefully your parents taught you to clean your teeth morning and night and this is a practice you should continue. But you will need to supplement this by using dental floss or small 'interdens' brushes to remove any food trapped between your teeth, which will reduce inflammation of the gums and other problems.

Daily regime

Have a good toothbrush, ideally a proper electric toothbrush with a head, which is changed regularly. Find a toothpaste that you like and dental floss. Clean your teeth morning and night and do it thoroughly, not just a cursory brush over. Take your time.

Using dental floss daily will reduce long-term build up around the bottom of the teeth and other more serious problems.

Annual regime

Find a good dentist, and ideally a dental hygienist within the same practice, then go to him or her on a regular basis. How regularly is something you will need to agree between you, your dentist and your wallet (if you are unable to find a national health dentist)

If you visit the hygienist you may well find that unless you have any serious or underlying problems you can see the hygienist every 4-6 months and the dentist as infrequently as once a year for a check-up. The hygienist will be able to help you with advice on brushing and flossing your teeth and how you can improve what you are doing every day.

Manicure/Pedicure

These are not words common to most men, but the health and tidiness of your nails is one of the things that women look at in a man and a pedicure can prevent issues such as ingrowing toenails.

Why is it important to look after nails?

Keeping your nails short, well cut and clean is a very visible sign that you care about your health and your grooming. Bitten or overlong dirty nails are a sign that you are nervous, distracted or that you do not care about your appearance and do not take care of yourself.

What regime should a Gentleman have?

Keep your nails short and tidy and ensure you have a good nailbrush to allow you to keep your nails clean.

Avoid bitten nails and if you work with your hands you my consider using a moisturiser around the nails to keep the skin in good condition.

What regime should I have for my feet?

Keep your toenails cut short but not too short and cut the nails straight across. Do not cut down the side of the nails as this can encourage sideways growth, which could develop into ingrowing toenails.

If you shower regularly you may omit to wash your feet every time. It is very important, if you play a lot of sport or if you suffer from sweaty feet, to wash your feet regularly to avoid athlete's foot, which is a fungal infection between the toes. It may also be a good idea to apply a medicated powder or spray to prevent or get rid of athlete's foot.

Preparing for that Big Date or Interview

Ensuring that you are properly groomed for a special event is not something that you can come to on the day. It is something that you need to think about and prepare for. Ensure that you have everything you need and use practiced and proven grooming practices rather than something you may have decided to try on the day.

Planning and preparing

Plan your grooming and practice everything you are going to do so that you know what you are doing. The morning before an important wedding or interview, or the evening before an important date, is not the time to be experimenting with a new face wash that you might be allergic to or a time to decide that you need a full 'facial' resulting in a face that looks like it has just been through five rounds with a heavyweight boxer.

Regime rather than last minute panic

Be aware of each of the elements – showering/bathing, washing your hair, shaving or trimming your beard, styling your hair, ensuring your nails are cut and clean and lastly applying a fragrance. Ensure you have everything you need: new razor blades, shampoo and conditioner, moisturiser and all the individual elements to ensure there is no last minute panic.

Allow enough time

Calculate how much time each element will take and ensure you have sufficient time to achieve all the elements and to do everything in a relaxed way so that everything happens smoothly.

Contrast scents and avoid a 'clash'

Think about the products that you use, ensure that you do not use multiple 'preparations' with different scents resulting in a 'clash' of scents as they fight each other.

Do not overload the fragrance!

Be subtle with your fragrance or cologne, apply your selected cologne to pressure points and heat points on your body. If you are using a good quality natural cologne the fragrance will last, and if it is properly selected it will tone in with your natural smell.

Be natural

If you have to work too hard to maintain a specific hairstyle you may be thinking too much about how you look so that you are not able to focus on the job in hand. Aim to create a natural look and one with which you feel comfortable.

Be a Perfect Gentleman!

Plan, practice and refine your grooming regime until it becomes second nature. Be natural and relaxed and be the Perfectly Groomed Gentleman.

The Mannered Gentleman

" Manners maketh man"

William of Wykeham

Why?

The world has changed and so have a great number of the social conventions that have existed for hundreds of years. People have become more selfish, with many adhering to a 'do what you want' attitude with no thought for consequences. More frequently people show little respect or manners, as they do not believe they will receive any in return. Both of these negative approaches become downward spirals of self-fulfilling prophecies.

Yet, manners are important; they are the social bonds that keep society ticking over. They show you have both grace and humility and an ability to think of others as well as yourself. They can bring a smile to someone's face and positively affect someone's day. And the more people that display manners the more that the negative mindset of society can slowly shift towards positivity. A Gentleman is an example to others and to himself.

We are not advocating some rigid code that breeds mindless obedience, what we are talking about is the social niceties and pleasantries that make all the difference and make things easier.

As we discussed in the earlier chapters on the core values and history, manners have a long history and are based on the developing rules of court. However, these were not limited to court but extended to every household across the land to build unity and commonality.

Most people think manners refer solely to our behaviour at the dinner table, and dining etiquette does take up a good part of this chapter, but it is far from all that manners entail. Let us start at the beginning.

The Basics – The Common Manners

We mentioned the Commons and Common manners in '*The Core of the Gentleman*' Chapter. The Common Manners are the simple things that we should use everyday and a gentleman always does.

Even if you only master the commons, that one thing will stand you head and shoulders above most others and will change your life.

Let's start with the basic and fundamental 'please' and 'thank you', words that should roll of your tongue effortlessly, frequently and genuinely. These words are an expression of humility and gratitude that date back to that key period in the gentleman's history, the middle ages and beyond.

It is gratitude that we as humans wish to receive. Our emotional cores are bolstered when our actions have been gratefully received. Words carry a great deal of meaning and value.

Moving beyond those basic words, the other key factor in good general manners is being considerate, in other words, thinking of others. This includes being punctual, opening doors for people, letting people get on and off public transport, offering your seat, helping people with their pram or luggage and even taking out the rubbish.

These little actions are all about being considerate and in today's world they are not often seen and sometimes regarded with suspicion. This is only because people have stopped showing consideration for others, and lost in their own world, unaware of the greater world. If we all start to be considerate then we start to change the world.

The other thing that shows a true gentleman with manners is the ability to admit when he is wrong. The words 'I'm Sorry' or indeed a genuine 'Excuse Me' is worth its weight in gold. How you say sorry depends on the nature of the problem. If you bump into someone then the words should be sufficient, but if it is something more serious then words backed with actions are essential. The only instance when a straight sorry might not be warranted is when there maybe legal implications, but those times should be obvious.

Common Manners are there to aid us with that first impression, not only to those with whom we are directly engaging, but also those observing and watching. Your good manners might mean someone else will follow your example and spread good manners around the world.

A Gentleman's Hints:

- Always remember that 'Please' and 'Thank You' are still magic words.

- Gratitude is the feeling - Grateful is the action. A gentleman becomes one through his actions.

- Remember to be considerate at all times. Keep this in the back of your mind.

- A gentleman is considerate, grateful and thoughtful.

Events

There are several key life events that a gentleman needs to be able to deal with in a well-mannered way. If you are looking for advice on Engagements & Weddings, that particular information can be found in the Romantic Gentleman Chapter.

During the Gentleman's life he will have to be prepared for many and all different circumstances. We have listed here traditional Western customs for these life events, though the basic gestures and formalities hold true.

Births

A birth is a time of great joy for the new parents and their close family. There are so many traditions around the birth of a child, which ones you will have to observe will depend on the parents and the gentleman's relationship with the family.

Upon hearing the news of the pregnancy, the gentleman should offer his congratulations. This should be done with a phone call, email or in the best possible manner with a hand written card.

Before the birth of the child, you might be invited to a 'baby shower'. This is a small party that is the formal announcement of the pregnancy. It is generally an all female affair, but in the modern world it is not unheard of for men to be invited. It is customary for the guests to bring a gift for the impending arrival.

Once the baby is born, a gentleman might be asked to 'wet the baby's head' and celebrate with the new father. This will involve some alcohol and generally gifts of cigars. In more recent years this is combined with the christening/naming ceremony as a celebratory event.

Depending on your closeness to the family, you might be invited to the religious ceremonial part of the christening/naming ceremony. Do observe the tenements of the place of worship that you are visiting.

It is generally a smart affair and a gentleman should wear a suit and tie for this event, though not as formal as he would wear for the office.

Giving a present is usual at these events and traditionally it used to be a bible, christening spoon, or some jewellery, but today it is more commonly personalised items that appreciate over time.

You might be offered the high honour of becoming the child's Godparent. This is a substantial undertaking with responsibility to offer love, support and friendship to the child as a baseline, and, if religious, to be the spiritual mentor for the child. Traditionally the Godparents would also be the legal guardians if anything happened to the parents, but this is not generally the case anymore.

Funerals

As the arrival of a baby is a time of great joy, a funeral can be a time of great sadness. It is also a time to celebrate the life of and show love to the deceased.

There are legal, religious and cultural aspects to this event. The legal requirements should be researched for your own individual requirements. The role you might have to take on will depend on your relationship with the deceased.

If you are Next of Kin, then you should inform people the sad news as soon as possible. Start with the key people and work outwards. You always use the phone as a preferred method of communication, email if necessary and handwritten letter or card if the relations are distant or strained.

Once those closest have been informed it is customary to place an advert in the newspaper. This will inform people of the death and provide details of the funeral.

The Undertaker will do a great deal of the work but will need input from the family.

Funerals can take many forms these days, be ready to inform people exactly what kind of event it will be, how formal and the requirements of the deceased.

The dress code for most funerals is smart; generally dark or black suit with a black or dark tie.

Always offer your condolences and support to those who are closest to the deceased. If you are a relation then be prepared to be fully supportive to your family and relations.

Always treat the ceremony with the seriousness and respect it deserves.

After the ceremony it is customary to attend another venue for refreshment. This is sometimes called a 'wake'. It can also take various forms, from somber and sad to loud and celebratory.

Former New York City Mayor, Rudolph Guillani once said that 'weddings are optional, funerals are compulsory' and as a gentleman that should hold true. You should always make the effort to attend the funerals you are invited to. It shows respect to those who have passed away.

Parties

One of the most common events that a gentleman attends is a party. Whether that is a formal dinner party, a casual affair, large group get-together or even a weekend style 'house party'.

Being a great guest is about being considerate. It is good manners to turn up to the party with a small gift for your hosts. General choices for these gifts are wine, flowers and chocolates, but can be more interesting choices such as plants, books and other small household items.

As a gentleman your job is to be considerate and helpful, if the party is informal then do offer to help out in the kitchen or serve drinks for other guests. At the end of the event it is good conduct to offer a lift home to people, if you are in a state to do so.

It is uncommon to send a thank you card, but a gentleman should send a thoughtful, hand written note to his hosts, as it will be gratefully appreciated.

Letter & Email Etiquette

Though letter writing is becoming a dying art with the advent of email, the principles of the letter can be applied to your email communication.

The speed and informality of email has caused some standards to slip and some major mistakes have been made. It is, therefore, a wise plan to treat your email as you would do a letter.

The Letter

It is correct form to write the full name, title/position and address of the recipient on the top right hand side of the page.

The date should be written below the address and should be written in full.

The letter needs to be addressed correctly:

Dear Sir/Madam - The Person is not known to you at all, or you know their position but not their name.

Dear Mr X or Miss/Ms/Mrs X - If you know the person's name but have not met them personally or it is a very formal communication.

Dear (First Name) - This form of address is used for people that you know and with whom you have regular communication.

If you are great friends then you can use the first name without a salutation.

After the greeting, one should place a line in bold typeface stating the subject of the letter.

The main body of the letter should be written in your own style but be clear and concise and contain all the relevant information.

The ending of the letter should correspond to the salutation:

If the salutation is formal, then the ending should be "yours faithfully", a space and then your full name.

If the salutation is semi-formal then the sign-off should be "yours sincerely", a space and then your full name.

If the salutation is informal then you can end in a number of ways. Such as "Kind regards" or "Best Wishes".

A full list of correct titles and correct forms of address can be found on the website in our resources section.

The Email

In an email the salutations and the endings should follow the same form as the letter.

It is exceptionally poor form to respond to an email without some form of salutation and 'sign-off', even if you are quickly responding to a friend. The email is neither a text message nor a short message via another form of communication, therefore should not be treated as one.

The Subject line of an email should be clear in its detail and if you are unknown to the person, it might be advisable to include your name.

> **A Gentleman's Hints:**
>
> A hand written letter or thank you note is now a pleasant surprise for someone in this digital age.
>
> - No matter what the communication a few lines of manners go an exceptionally long way.
> - Always personally sign your physical letters.
> - Do not send emails all in one case. It shows poor form.
> - Refrain from sending chain letters or jokes.

Digital Etiquette

We live in an increasingly digital age; where communication is fast and immediate; our lives are displayed on the social networks and we can talk to friends and family over the whole globe. That does not mean that we have an excuse to forget manners and etiquette.

The most frequent digital device that invades our lives is the mobile phone. The ability to speak to anyone anywhere has it advantages, but also comes with a few serious issues.

The first issue is that people believe that they are in a phone bubble when they are conversing and will talk about all matters when anyone and everyone can hear them. It is a frequent occurrence while travelling on public transport to learn the entire life-story of a nearby passenger. This can include business secrets and insider information being discussed on a mobile phone within earshot of an entire train carriage. Take some time to think about where you are and what you are talking about on the telephone; you never know who is listening. If you must take a phone call, remove yourself to a place where you cannot be overheard, or ask to call them back at a later time.

Recently, before we had mobile phones, we had fixed line phones and answer machines. We could not immediately answer calls, and we had to wait to make them. They did not disturb meetings, meals, theatre performances or many other events and experiences. Now it is not just phone calls, but also texts, emails and other communications. A gentleman thinks about those around him, therefore he will take his time to answer phone calls and respond to emails and other communications. He will not disturb events for the quick chat to discuss the football score.

We at the Perfect Gentleman recommend you place your phone on vibrate at all times unless you are expecting an urgent call or are away from it whilst doing a task. Never answer your phone when you are at an event or engaged in a conversation or a date.

One other issue that is becoming a frequent occurrence in the modern world is the lack of awareness of one's surroundings whilst buried in a phone or other electronic device. People wander along the street, head hunched over the phone and not looking at anything going on around them. We refer to this phenomena as 'The Bubble'. The personal safety aspect of this is exceptionally worrying, and then there is the lack of consideration for your fellow pedestrians. It is becoming increasingly common to witness accidents and other minor confrontations because of this phenomenon. A gentleman is always aware of his surroundings and considerate to his fellow walking humans.

We are online all the time, whether that be Facebook, Twitter, LinkedIn or any number of other social platforms. They are amazingly useful for such things as business communication, social interactions and marketing purposes. The current and younger generations have an attitude that it is all right to display anything and everything. Alternatively people view the digital realm as different to the physical realm and place things on the digital realm that they would never do in the physical.

As with everything that goes with being a perfect gentleman, he needs to take into consideration his public perception. We are putting ourselves on display in this digital realm, therefore it is wise to imagine that you are the leader of a country or a role model appearing in the press everyday being judged on your behaviour by all. How would you change your public and digital behaviour if that were the case? A gentleman thinks in that way. Wherever he is, at whatever time, he behaves with courtesy and manners, abiding by the core values.

Start by following these simple rules with regard to the digital world and you will cover most of the situations.

Dining Etiquette

When most people think of manners and etiquette they think of Table Manners. Most people will be familiar with their parents commanding them to behave at the dinner table with common refrains such as 'Sit up Straight' or 'Do not talk with your mouth full'. But dining etiquette is far more complex than these homilies trotted out by our parents. The manners and etiquette of dining have been around for as long as we have eaten collectively, it even predates Tables themselves. When the tribe used to sit huddled round a roaring fire with one pot containing the evening meal there would be a hierarchy in the tribe as to who would be able to eat the choicest pieces of meat. This was the earliest instance of dining etiquette and it has only become more complicated.

It is amazing how a few table manners can create an excellent impression. Whether it is a dinner date with your beautiful partner or a business lunch with your boss, displaying behaviour more suited to the barn will not get you into her heart or into the boardroom. Whereas great manners should be so graceful, that they do not appear to have happened at all, effortless ease.

Preparation

As with all things a little preparation goes a long way. Ask yourself some key questions: Where are you going? What are you eating? Who are you with? When is the meal?

The venue is important. Is it a banquet, a Michelin starred restaurant, a favourite local haunt or afternoon tea? It will dictate such things as your dress code, but more importantly what to expect and what is expected of you.

The type and style of food has a profound effect on your manners. You do not want to be daunted with chopsticks at a Chinese meal or figuring out which hand to use at a Middle Eastern banquet. (The correct hand is the Right Hand)

The company at your meal is what makes any meal a fully rounded out experience, so it is best to understand with whom you are dining. Whether it is as simple as your family or a more complex mix of clients and staff, it is exceptionally helpful to know. As a gentleman's duty is to make people feel at ease, he should anticipate issues such as the food intolerances of his children or preventing the serving of alcohol to Muslim guests.

A little preparation can make a great deal of difference to your whole dining experience.

A Gentleman's Hints:

- Preparation is key, ask about the Where, What and Who.

- Anticipation is key to effortless ease. If you think something might be a problem do something to counter it.

- When selecting a restaurant, remember your guests' food/drink requirements and any other limitations that your party might have, such as wheelchair use.

Before the Food

Even before you receive a drink or pick up a menu there are things to think about.

If you are in a restaurant, it is considered polite to seat ladies so that they are facing the restaurant. If it is a larger group then men and women should be sat in alternate seats and partners/husbands/wives should not be sat next to each other, though opposite sides of a table is acceptable. Ladies should be seated first by the gentleman and in larger groups the gentleman should help seat the lady to his right before seating himself. If it is a formal occasion, one might have to wait till all the ladies are present before taking your seat, and in some cases, if there is an honoured guest, you will wait for them to be present.

Tradition dictates that if there is thirteen for dinner an extra place setting will be set and in some places a figure or statue is placed as the fourteenth guest. In the Savoy hotel there is a wooden cat that is used for this tradition.

If the situation is one where you do not know the guests around you then introduce yourself as soon as you are in your place, this is especially true of the guests either side of you.

In certain cultures and places 'Grace' is said before the meal is served. It is polite to respect the wishes of the host, even if it is not your beliefs.

Do not start your meal until all at the table are served and the host, or your lady guest, picks up their cutlery to eat, the exception is if the host insists you begin.

During the meal

During the meal it is unacceptable to remove a suit jacket if you have one on and depending on the dress code for the establishment or invitation it will be unacceptable to remove your tie as well.

Elbows should be kept off the table during all the food courses but during post meal conversation and coffee then you can place them on the table.

If you need to excuse yourself from the table for whatever reason then say to your guest, host or the people either side you 'Would you please excuse me?' and then leave. Do not disturb any conversation when you return.

If a lady leaves the table, it is now old fashioned to rise, but it is quite acceptable to rise from your seat when she returns and if necessary help her back into her seat.

THE TABLE

The Napkin

A piece of etiquette that dates back to the Middle Ages, when it was brought back to Europe from Knights returning from the Crusades. It was a piece of cloth, and in some cases it was the tablecloth itself, that was there to wipe messy fingers and clean the mouth from all the food that was consumed mostly with the hands.

The napkin now is a piece of cloth, generally starched linen, which is placed in your table setting for your use during the meal. The napkin will either be in the centre of your place setting or on your left and frequently on the side plate.

Once you are seated, take the napkin discretely from the table, fold it in half and place it across your lap. If you are being exceptionally well mannered the fold should be towards your lap and can be placed either across your whole lap or just across one leg.

The napkin should be used to wipe your fingers if necessary and dab gently around your mouth.

If you need to leave the table for any reason then fold your napkin and place it on your seat. When you have finished your meal you should fold your napkin and place it to the left of your plate or in front of you if the plates have been cleared. It is exceptionally impolite to scrunch your napkin up and leave it anywhere.

The Glasses

The minefield of dining grows ever more complex with the glassware that can appear on a formal dining table. Glassware has developed over time to create the perfect glass for most drinking occasions. Here we will only cover the main ones that appear at a lunch or dinner table. In a restaurant, if you are lucky and the waiting staff is excellent, you will never have to worry, but that is not the same for a gathering at a home or hosting your own party. All drinking glasses are generally placed on the top right-hand side of your dining place setting.

The water glass is generally the only one without a stem, if it does have a stem it is usually the largest glass on the table. It is usually placed nearest to you but furthest right of the setting.

Champagne or sparkling wine is served in a glass called a flute and like its namesake is a tall thin glass. The glass will also have a long thin stem. The shape is to keep the bubbles there for longer. It is usually placed on the top right of the group of wine glasses.

White wine is served in a rounded but slender glass, which generally has a shorter stem than other wine glasses. It is placed front left of the wine

A red wine glass is the same shape as the white wine one, but is generally larger and more rounded, this gives the wine room to 'breathe'.

Chilled wine and champagne glasses should be held and drunk using only the stem, this means that your wine is prevented from the warmth of your hands.

Wine glasses should only ever be filled about halfway and water and champagne about three quarters full.

A Gentleman's Quick Guide Wine

Ordering: If you have little or no knowledge of wines then do not be afraid to ask the waiter/bartender/staff, or if the place is sufficiently formal then the Sommelier *(som-el-ee-ay)*. It is his job to know what is good, what you can afford or indeed provide some pointers.

If you wish to know more then start by tasting wine and picking up a number of helpful guidebooks or websites (we have a couple listed in the online resources section for this book) Always remember the grape variety and where it came from.

When it comes to tasting the wine then the modern custom is that the person paying the bill should taste the wine. Due to historical roles, the man is usually offered the taste of the wine, this maybe inaccurate and he should indicate to whom the first taste should go.

When the wine is opened, if it has a cork it is usual to smell the cork to check for leakage. The waiter will then pour a small amount into your glass. Pick the glass up by the stem and give it a quick swirl and then sniff the aroma. Take a sip and let it flush around your mouth a little. If the wine is 'corked' (where air has gotten into the bottle and spoiled the wine) then it will have a distinctive rotting aroma and a vinegary taste. The waiter will generally confirm this and replace the wine. It is infrequent in modern wine, but more common in older wines.

It is perfectly acceptable at this point, if you do not like the wine at all, or believe something is wrong with it, to have it replaced.

As for the wine to go with the meal, it is standard convention that white wine goes with fish or light meals and red wine accompanies meat or heavy courses or meals. However, this is now frequently subverted; so do not expect this except at the most formal of parties or restaurants.

There may be an instance where you are with people who do not drink alcohol. In which case you might need to look at alternative drink choices.

Cutlery & Plates

The second confusing area is plates and cutlery, otherwise known as the 'place setting'.

As you sit down in front of you will be a set of cutlery and some plates and some glasses. We have covered the glasses, which will sit on the top right hand side of the place setting.

On the left hand side of the place setting there will be a small plate; this is called your 'side plate'. It should have a small knife and possibly your napkin upon it. This small plate is used for your bread and any small discarded items from your main meal, such as bones or shells. Your side plate will be removed after the main course. The small knife is your butter knife and used very simply to place butter on your bread.

The main area in front of you will generally be clear of any plates but will have a swathe of cutlery. The centre area may contain a large decorative plate, called a 'charger plate'. This is generally used for pure decoration but can also be used as the base plate for your starter course; it will certainly be removed at some point.

The swathe of cutlery can be quite daunting if it is fully set out for a multi-course meal. Happily, there is one simple rule that is easily followed with cutlery; work from the outside in.

The main cutlery will be set horizontal to the table edge and parallel to each other. Forks will be on the left and the knives and spoons will be on the right. The cutting side of the knives will always face the plate.

Sometimes the cutlery for the pudding course is placed horizontally above the plate, often due to lack of space on the table.

Generally in order of size from smallest to largest, the cutlery goes; pudding, starter and main. If you are served soup this will be the cutlery furthest to the right-hand side.

A Gentleman's Hints:

- Never hold your cutlery when you are not actively using it to cut or eat your food. If you wish to talk then place you cutlery down on the plate.

- If you are resting during the course, place your cutlery on the plate separately as if the hands of the clock are at 7 and 4 on the clock face. If it is one-piece cutlery place it at about 3 on the clock face.

- When you have finished your meal, place your cutlery together and leave them at 5 on the clock face.

- In some cultures, using your hands to eat is acceptable. If this is the case then only use your right hand, as your left is considered 'dirty'.

- If in a different culture or foreign land then it is probably advisable to follow the lead of your host.

Business Meals

Whether it is lunch or dinner a business meal is an excellent way to display impeccable manners, which is rather a paradox as your manners should not be visible. Business meals are a great opportunity to discuss matters in an informal environment.

- Always turn up early for the reservation.

- Turn off your phone whilst at the meal.

- Get settled in and order food before getting to the business conversation.

- Always avoid messy or difficult foods

- Order a smaller meal than normal, you want to talk business not be a glutton.

- If you are the host, pay the bill.

As a general rule, no matter if you are in a restaurant, bar, private function or anywhere where you are served or waited upon. Always be polite and considerate to the staff, they are doing a job and need to be recognised and appreciated.

Saying Goodbye

A gentleman is always polite and at the end of the day, when it comes time to leave the party, meal or any other encounter, he will always say goodbye, initially to the host/hostess, thanking them for their hospitality. He will also always go round and say an appropriate goodbye to all the guests he has met where possible.

Remember the Thank You Card.

Manners start out becoming a conscious effort, having to think about every little thing you do; remembering every 'please' and 'thank you' and which knife to use at which meal or indeed not to take that call over dinner. Over time, with practice, they start to blend into the background and become easier. Practice makes the Perfect Gentleman.

THE BUSINESS GENTLEMAN

" A business absolutely devoted to service will have only one worry about profits. They will be embarrassingly large."

Henry Ford

The Rise of the Business Man

Trade has existed since Man realised he could not do everything alone, but for centuries the general business figure was predominately a lone trader in a city, plying his baking or blacksmith work, or a supplier cross between trading post or cities. There were a few organised groups of traders with some dating back as far as the mid 13th Century.

The real rise of the businessman coincided with the explosion of international trade during the renaissance and the rise of colonialism. The City of London became the hub of international trade and with it came the rise of the company and its support services of banks, insurance, lawyers and other services.

The first global mega-corporation was the East India Company, which was established in 1600 by Queen Elizabeth I. It was a company that had a swathe of directors and a plethora of managers and with it the businessman was truly born. But still these pioneers of business frequently had to resort to force of arms to get the job done and therefore the old military codes of behaviour still came through and every businessman was also expected to be a gentleman.

Not until the Industrial Revolution did the current model of the Business Man that we recognise today come into being and there was infrequent need for a man of business to drop his pen and pick up his pistol. The world became smaller and the boardroom was becoming the battlefield and yet throughout this period, manners and etiquette were expected to be adhered to.

Throughout the last hundred years, business has changed and no more so than in the last two decades. Alhough this is neither an economics book nor a business school lecture, we cannot talk about the business man today without mentioning the complete lack of faith the general populace has with the 'City' institutions, large corporations and general business behaviour today. Not a day has passed since 2008 without a tale of greed, poor ethics, mis-selling, or any of the other morally ambivalent business practices.

We are not here to rake over the past but to instil a vision for the future. Perhaps businesses, and those people who run them, should look to the past and the more gentlemanly conduct of yesteryear. Make long term plans not based on quarterly stock market needs; make decisions not just for bottom line profit but for the good of the company and the employees within it; help those to start on their path and those who need to help when they end theirs; take what you need, not everything that you can grasp along the way; make a deal based on a handshake and keep to it. Most of these stem from the code of chivalry and our core values, but they are true of all men and women across the business world.

Success

Success is a very subjective thing; each person has his or her own version of it. Whether it is the billionaire lifestyle of private jets and private islands, or the ability to be comfortable enough to provide well for your family, everyone is different.

Whatever his goals in life, a gentleman should strive to be the best he can be and as successful as he desires to be.

As a gentleman he should certainly 'walk the walk' and never just 'talk the talk'. A gentleman, no matter how successful, will never show off or display his superiority nor will he envy the success of others no matter how far from that point he is. As a gentleman always knows that things can change quite rapidly in one's fortunes.

The success a gentleman should strive for is the success of trying to better himself, the lives of those closest to him and the world at large.

The Corporate Gentleman vs The Entrepreneur Gentleman

We are expected to decide what we wish to become at an increasingly young age. Western/Modern education is predicated on our making choices about subjects at various and exceptionally early points in our education trajectory. Our path becomes increasingly narrow the further up the education ladder we climb, but the working world has become increasingly broad and we are now in a world were flexibility and continuous knowledge acquisition are the keys to success.

The working world has changed drastically, from the feudal to the industrial to the current information economy that is aided by technology. Gone are the days of joining one company and staying there for your working life; the average time at one company now is three to four years. We are no longer in an era where starting your own business is considered beneath a gentleman. There is no one path that suits all, we are all individuals and even the paths may cross and change along the road.

What to choose, in simple terms the corporate path is steady, generally safe and if you do your job well and climb the ladder successfully, exceptionally rewarding. The entrepreneurial or self-employed path can be certainly more risky and more challenging, but can be the most successful and rewarding path of all.

Either path suits different character traits, one thing a gentleman should do is learn his strengths a weaknesses. There are many different personality tests on the market, which will give you a guide to who you are and what you are capable of.

The gentleman can thrive in either environment; it is about choice, personality, desire and a sense of belonging.

> **A Gentleman's Hints:**
>
> * Learn your strengths & weaknesses: Take a Test or two.
>
> * Set Goals – Begin with the end in mind and work backwards.
>
> * Do your research before you choose. Perhaps ask to intern at an establishment to see how things work and whether you like the work.
>
> * There are many career paths, never feel boxed in by one. If you do not like something, move on.
>
> * There is no such thing as an overnight success, no matter what the media states. It will take hard work to achieve your dreams, but it will be worth it.

Confidence

One of the core values of the gentleman, as mentioned previously, is self-confidence and this is especially true of the business world.

Confidence helps people believe in you as a businessman. If we honestly believe we can deliver that contract or excel in the job then the client or our employer will have faith that we can.

It is a true fact of business that the confidence that the customer has in you or your business can be crucial to your success. If your customer believes in you then you can create a strong and loyal following, which can spur you on to greater success.

Go back and look at the section on self-confidence in "The Core of the Gentleman" chapter.

Skills – The Business Education

Throughout history a gentleman was expected to have a broad and diverse set of skills, which were often combat related. In today's society the ability to fight with a variety of weapons is not so relevant, but in the modern battlefield of the business world a diverse set of skills is a valuable asset.

We all need the basic skills of the ability to read, write, do basic mathematics and hold a conversation with our fellow man or woman. Those are the core building blocks that build the solid foundations of Gentlemen. Beyond that we are in the age of information and working predominately in a knowledge based economy and therefore we need to constantly acquire, polish and refine our quiver of skills.

Knowledge can be gained in a number of ways through formal education, such as schools and universities and other such institutions. It can be garnered through registered specialist institutions, which will give focus and career path education. There is informal education, whether that is via books, videos, seminars, courses, workshops and coaching that gives you different and some times more practical information. Whichever path or combination you choose, do not forget that education should never stop. The Perfect Gentleman is always learning.

What skills are important in the modern world and which ones should we focus on first? Below is a list of core and advanced skills that will help you succeed in whichever area of business you wish to pursue.

We at the Perfect Gentleman will help you through some of these skills in this book and through our website and other products. Some aspects are beyond our remit, but we have some up to date recommendations on our website or you can choose to do some research for yourself.

Core Skills

These broad core skills might seem simplistic but they will serve you well throughout your career. They are sweeping and made up of several components.

- Communication: The ability to speak, write and communicate your thoughts and ideas, clearly and sometimes with humour. This includes the ability to converse with anyone; negotiation skills

- Social/Emotional Intelligence: This encompasses everything from being able to build rapport with people, build teams, leadership skills, delegation abilities and other skills that involve people.

- Strategy: The ability to look at a situation, evaluate and analyze it and then be able to plan and set goals for future success.

- Financial Intelligence: This goes beyond basic mathematics. It is about understanding how cash works in a business and the differences between income and expenditure and how money flows through business and life.

- Time Management: One of the key factors in business and in life is the ability to manage your time effectively. This skill is simple to understand but difficult to master, and mastering it will empower you to achieve great things.

Advanced Skills

These are more advance skills that are more specialized and in most instances require a more concentrated level of education.

- Languages: We are in a global world, your next client might be Chinese or your next employee might be Mexican. It behoves you to be able to speak their language, in fact any language. We recommend the following Six as ones that cover the world: English; Mandarin (Chinese); Spanish; Arabic; French; Russian.

- Sales: The life blood of any business is Sales and yet a fraction of universities and a handful of business schools teach any sales training. You are always selling something, so it is best to learn how.

- Marketing: Though Sales and Marketing go hand in hand they are different disciplines and the knowledge about how to present the best case for you, your company or your product to the outside world is essential. In fact, a great deal of what we do in The Perfect Gentleman is about presenting a great Brand You.

- Public Speaking & Presentation: No matter what position you hold, whether you are corporate focused or entrepreneurially bound, you will have to stand up and speak to people and make presentations. Learning the ability to wow people, rather than put them to sleep, will make you soar above others.

- Computer Skills: We live in a digital world, where technology permeates every aspect of our lives. To survive you need to understand the basics, not everyone is going to be a master coder or SEO expert, but understanding the fundamentals is a good place to begin, then find something that you like and keep studying it.

These are a limited but key selection of skills that we believe will make a difference and take any Gentleman to the heights of success.

Getting in the Door

The first step on any path is getting in the door and there are three simple steps that will help you secure that first step, or perhaps new start.

Introductions

'It is not what you know, it is who you know.'

Anonymous

There is a game that you might have come across called 'Six Degrees of Kevin Bacon', which is about seeing how close an actor is to having starred with Kevin Bacon. It is based on the theory that everyone is connected by no more than a chain of six people. If that is true you can get to almost anyone. The question is how?

You need to introduce yourself, which could come in the direct form of a Handshake (as we discuss below), or you might need to go through a friend. With the proliferation of Social Networks, such as LinkedIn, this connection maze has become much easier, but we still need to connect.

A Gentleman's Hints:

- Always be polite, to the point and make sure you have done your homework.

- If communicating directly to someone, let the person know who you are, why you wish to connect and that you value their time. If someone introduced you, let them know who and why.

- If you are asking to be introduced through a contact, ask politely and tell your contact what you wish to gain from the introduction, as it is their reputation you are drawing on. If they decline, say thank you and move on. If they agree to make the introduction, say 'Thank You' and remember to do something nice for them if it benefits you greatly.

- If you are asked to do an introduction and agree to do it, then contact both parties and state clearly why you are making the introduction and who the people are, but keep it short and simple. Let the people communicate directly as soon as possible.

- General rules; Do your homework, say thank you and if appropriate reciprocate where you can.

The Curriculum Vitae (CV) or Resume

The history of the Resume is 500 years old, the great Leonardo da Vinci wrote the first professional resume. It has developed over time, from the basic letter of introduction to the formal structure that it is now. It has adapted with technology with video and multimedia playing an ever-increasing part.

What is the difference between a Resume and a CV, simply put, not a great deal. In most countries they are the same thing. In the UK, America, Canada and Australia, and a few other countries, the difference is simple; a resume is a much shorter document than a CV.

Do we still need them? Well the death of the CV has been speculated since the late 1980s, but the document in various forms is still here. It is the simplest way to communicate your skills, knowledge and experience.

A Gentleman's Hints:

- Some general points: Tell the Truth; Keep it Clean, Clear and Simple; Make sure the spelling and grammar is correct.

- Study a number of formats and frameworks and use one that feels comfortable for you.

- Have a standard CV but then customize it to each job you are applying for, it might take extra time but it is worth the effort.

- Keep your CV and Social Media profiles up to date.

- Remember to add references, and do let the people who you are using for references know that is what you have done.

- The CV should be relatively impersonal.

- To highlight your personality and other information place it all in the Covering Letter or Email.

- Never send anyone your CV without them asking for it.

Interview

It is scary meeting someone face to face, being put on display like an ornament and then being questioned about yourself just adds to the pressure.

The interview is generally the key element to any job; people 'buy' people. You need to display your very best and honest YOU. Never forget your core gentleman's values and you will not go far wrong.

A Gentleman's Hints:

- Dress conservatively, even for a creative company. You have seven seconds to make that first impression.

- 'Be Confident', even if you do not feel it at that time.

- Shake hands, maintain eye contact and smile.

- Sit still and keep calm. Moving and fidgeting makes you appear difficult and hiding something.

- DO YOUR RESEARCH: About the company, the job you are applying for, the people you are going to be working for and, if you can, the interviewer.

- Listen first, then ask relevant questions. This will show your engagement and attention.

- Be Honest, saying that you do not know the answer is better than winging it.

- Write a follow up email or hand-written note within 24 hours, and make sure that your spelling and grammar are correct.

- Never Ever Burn Bridges.

Handshakes, Greetings & Business Cards

The glue of business is people and expanding your network of people is essential, the first contact is essential from offering your hand in hearty greeting, getting the correct introduction and presenting you business card. These are all key elements in making the first impression a resounding success.

The Handshake

There are number of potential origins of the humble handshake but the most commonly used one dates as far back as Ancient Greece, where the right hand (the general weapon bearing hand) was extended to prove that you were not carrying weapons and that there was no intention of harm to one another.

It is now done as a greeting, part of agreeing to a deal, as congratulations on some success, as a sign of sportsmanship and in parting.

Both genders can shake hands depending on the cultural requirements and implications, for instance in Russia shaking a Lady's hand can be considered impolite. In cultures where it is inappropriate then a nod or a short bow is best.

If you are greeting women, it is now a little outdated to kiss the hand of the lady, but can be very dashing in a non-business situation. If you are an established colleague or friend then the 'air kiss' has become an alternative greeting.

A Gentleman's Hints:

- In the majority of cases the handshake should be done barehanded.

- In most Western/Anglophone countries a firm handshake is preferred.

- In Arabic and Asian cultures a weaker handshake is the preference and mostly the senior person should initiate the handshake.

- If you are shaking hands, it should be for about 3-5 seconds, smile and keep eye contact the whole time.

Greetings and Introductions

' *...perhaps you'll be good enough to give us your real name, rank and serial number.*'

Richard Burton – Where Eagles Dare

It goes without saying that we are constantly introducing ourselves or greeting people on a daily basis; whether it is in the formal context with a new business contact, a social connection or with the maître d' at a restaurant. It is a sign of recognition and acknowledgement and perhaps even friendship and even esteem. In some instances even that of acceptance into a social group or hierarchy.

Whether it is a handshake, a bow, a cheek kiss or even a 'Namaste', the salutation usually follows it. In English this can be the simple 'Hello' or 'Good Morning' (or variations depending on the time of day) or the equivalent in your native language or the language of the person you are greeting. Then the conversation can commence.

The first time you met some one your Introduction is important, getting your name across and learning the other persons name is key. As Dale Carnegie once said '...a person's name is to that person the sweetest sound in any language', as a gentleman one should take care and listen to someone's name and use it. If you did not hear correctly the name the first time out then, do ask the person to repeat it.

A Gentleman's Hints:

- Greet with a handshake or the appropriate gesture, smile and maintain eye contact.

- If you are greeting a non-English speaker and you know the correct greeting, do use it.

- If you are greeting using the 'air' or 'cheek' kiss and you are not sure of the appropriate number (they do vary drastically across cultures) follow the lead of the person you are greeting.

- State your name clearly and how you wish to be addressed – if your name is complicated or long, do repeat it.

- If you miss the persons name do not hesitate to ask them to repeat it.

The Business Card

The Business card came from the merger of Trade Cards and Visiting cards and developed into the handy little items we carry today to display our contact details and our brand.

Visiting cards originated in China in the 15th Century and developed into a very formal piece of social etiquette in Europe in the 17'h,18th and 19th Centuries. They were the way to announce your visit to the head of the household and to promote yourself around court.

Trade Cards started to appear in London in the 17th Century. They served as advertisements to tell potential customers the range of services provided and directions through the confusing mostly unsigned streets of London.

The modern Business card is the international way to exchange contact details. It is simple, convenient and easy to share.

The customs that dictate the presentation and use of business cards do vary with different cultures around the world, but we will cover this in the International Gentleman chapter.

With the ever-increasing digital age and connectivity via social networks, printed business cards are on the decline. This may be the case amongst the more technically adept people, but a great business card is also a key talking point and works where the Internet may not.

A Gentleman's Hints:

- Always keep at few business cards with you. You never know when or where you might need them.

- Your business card is a reflection of you or your company's personality and therefore it should be designed with care.

- Printing of business cards nowadays is remarkably cheap; if possible, and if appropriate, a gentleman should have a personal card and a business card.

- Always take a business card with care, look at it, read it and if there is something to make comment on, feel free to do so.

Networking with Ease

' The Richest people in the world look for and build networks, everyone else looks for work.'

Robert Kiyosaki

No matter what the technological advances and increases in online social networking, people still form bonds and develop relationships through face to face contact. Real world connections make for real world business growth, as someone once said, 'the bigger your Rolodex, the bigger your business'.

It is about repeatedly positioning yourself at the centre of your business world and building your personal relationships and influence.

The Perfect Gentleman is a consummate networker; he knows how to 'work a room' and make everyone feel important.

Never stop expanding your network and meeting new people. You never know where that handshake or cocktail party will take you.

A Gentleman's Hints:

- Always carry business cards with you.

- Keep Smiling – it makes you approachable.

- If you want to remember someone's name easily, repeat it in the conversation with him or her at least three times, and make sure that you introduce him or her to someone else.

- Listen first. If someone is talking, let them talk and do not interrupt, your question can wait.

- Never brag or bluster.

- If you find it difficult to start conversation or want an easy opening question, ask about holidays. Most people have good memories about them or are looking forward to them and talking about them puts them in a cheerful disposition.

- Need to move on, excuse yourself politely by either refreshing your drink or stating you need to speak to other people and do not want to hold them up doing the same.

- At networking events: Arrive early and leave early.

- When drinking or eating, only drink and eat a very small amount. Quaffing the free booze and scoffing the canapés is not the way of the gentleman. Noel Coward once said that if you stay still at a party everyone would pass you eventually. If you are nervous or not on your best form, then this is an excellent tactic.

- If you are not feeling well or really not on form then think about not attending, you need to show your best face.

- If you have a specialized area and you always network in that area, do at least one networking event every other month that has nothing what so ever to do with your industry. You will be surprised by what occurs.

- If you want to keep in contact with someone then drop the person a quick note or email within 24 hours of your meeting.

Work & Life in the Digital Age

The world is always switched on; it is watching and listening, demanding attention and a desire to be fed information. We are firmly in the Digital Age, with all its pros and cons, but how as a Gentleman do you act in business and life in the 24-hour world?

The Mobile Phone

It is hard to remember now that it was only just a few years ago when you could not quickly call your business meeting to tell them you might be late, whilst on route and stuck in traffic. The mobile has become as essential as your wallet; indeed it might even start to replace it.

Yet the mobile is just a tool, it maybe an exceptionally smart one with enough computing power to send man to the moon, but at the end of the day it is a device to make your life easier, not to block out that life.

A Gentleman's Hints:

- In a Meeting, turn the phone on silent or off.

- If perhaps you are expecting an urgent call during a meeting, let the people you are with know.

- If you have to take the call, step away and give both the person you are with and the person you are speaking to privacy.

- If you are on the phone in public, be aware of what you are saying. You could inadvertently give away a company secret or a sensitive piece of information.

- Never ever use your phone to text, email or post onto Facebook whilst in a meeting, not only is it hugely disrespectful to the people you are with, you cannot give your full attention to the meeting and you might miss a vital piece of information.

- You do not have to take the call the moment it comes in; you can always call back.

- If you are leaving a message never assume that the person will recognise your voice, so leave your name and a clear message with your number.

- If you have been left a voicemail, do respond as promptly as you can or acknowledge receipt with a text message before following up with a phone call.

Email

The business letter is pretty much a thing of the past; email is the business communication of choice for the modern gentleman and yet we treat the email with a casualness that we reserve for text messages to friends.

The email, to all intents and purposes, is a letter that is digitally sent. It is quicker and more personal, but that should not mean that you treat it with any less importance than you would do a hand written letter.

A Gentleman's Hints:

- Take care with spelling, grammar and the greeting and ending of your email. Always think formal first.

- Unless you are good friends, your emails should be not be casual in tone or one line in length. It shows a level of casualness and thoughtlessness.

- Take the time to respond properly, a well thought out email is important.

- Set up prepared responses, so that you can send out emails quickly. An acknowledgement will buy you some time.

- Unless you are best friends, never send jokes, indecent images or anything inappropriate.

- Check the list of recipients before hitting that send button.

Social Media

The Billionaire investor Warren Buffet once said that he thought people in his employee should act like they would appear on the front page of the newspaper every day and display behaviour that their grandparents would be proud of. This translates especially well to the world of social media.

All our activity on social media is a public profile of who we are, what we do and believe in and how we work. You never know who might be able to view your Facebook photos of your misbehaviour and how that might affect your job prospects or that career in politics later in life.

A Gentleman's Hints:

- If you do not want people to know about it, do not place it on a social media site.

- Your Business Profiles should always be up to date.

- Be aware of what others post or say about you, most websites let you know when people talk about you and you can approve most posts that include you.

- If you are a regular poster, keep it honest with your character.

- Remember the law extends to social media, remember what you post about others.

Business Meetings

Meetings are the bane of the business world. Some are exceptionally necessary and some are just there for the sake of getting in the room. We all need the face-to-face interactions that meetings bring, but they have almost become the joke that will not die.

A Gentleman's Hints:

- Set an agenda or purpose: have a list of items that you are going to cover and do not go 'off topic'.

- Meetings have a start and an end time. Almost always keep it short.

- Set a rhythm, set regular meetings at regular days and times.

- Be Punctual and prepared, no one wants to wait for you to arrive or to muck around trying to get your papers together.

- Listen and do not interrupt, your turn will come.

- Make sure you address people correctly.

- Keep Minutes and Log Next Actions with who needs to do what.

- Have meetings while standing; people do not dawdle if they are standing.

- Keep it positive, suggest solutions and never judge.

- Make sure you post the notes and review.

- TURN OFF THE PHONE

Presentations & Speaking

It is a fact of modern business life that you will have to make a presentation or three, and the more senior you are the more likely you are going to have to speak for the company. Both of these similar tasks are daunting to the novice but with some simple skills and tips, the gentleman can be the perfect presenter.

We have all been in a presentation where we are suffering a slow death by PowerPoint presentation, or the speaker is droning on without any thought for his audience.

As humans we have imparted information for millennia by a tried and tested means and that is by telling stories. These engage the audience and get the message across. It does not matter whether you are discussing the quarterly figures or speaking at the annual conference, the story will engage your audience and prevent them nodding off over their notebooks.

Think how your presentation can become a story. Is your quarterly report a tale of rescuing the damsel of profit form the clutches of the rascal of bad sales? Anything can be made into a tale.

A Gentleman's Hints:

- If you must use a slide show, make sure you use mainly pictures and that all text is 30-point font or greater.

- Never read the slides or turn your back on your audience.

- Breathe In and Slow Down. Most people speak too fast; slow down and take your time. Breathe In through your nose only, it slows you down and gives you time. The Queen speaks like this.

- Maintain eye contact with your audience.

- Be entertaining, think about humour, passion and movement. Remember it is not a talent show.

- Practice, Practice, Practice. You can never have enough.

- NO JARGON. You never know who is in the audience so do not assume that they know the jargon you are using. Explain it simply and clearly. 'I had a Nocturnal Disturbance' is not as effective as 'I have a dream.'

- Speak to the back of the room as clearly as you can.

- Most of all, have fun!

This is a fraction of the skills and information that can make you become the Perfect Business Gentleman. There are shelves of books and piles of magazines that are filled with all manner of interesting and relevant business information. We have just scratched the surface, some resources and key books are listed on our website, along with our advanced courses and our regular articles. (www.theperfectgentleman.tv/BPGresources/)

THE TRAVELLING GENTLEMAN

" The World is a book, and those who do not travel read only a page. "

Saint Augustine

Maintaining a calm and stylish outlook when travelling is the mark of a true Gentleman.

However easy you may make it look, travelling can be difficult and challenging, particularly if you have no experience. So we have gathered together the wisdom and experience from the Perfect Gentlemen team's many years of international travel (both business and pleasure) and condensed it into this chapter.

Getting there...

Luggage

It is likely that you will need to have a range of luggage suitable for everything from short trips to the full two-week holiday.

If you are only away for a few days try to pack everything you need into carry-on bags. It will save valuable time not having to wait at the carousel when you arrive at your destination.

Be sure to check and double check the airlines policy on the size and number of bags you are allowed to carry. Many airlines will not check the size of your carry-on bags until you arrive at the departure gate and at that point you will have to pay a heavy penalty for putting it into the hold in addition to the delay on arrival.

For a short business trip a suit carrier is ideal. It allows you to flat pack suits and shirts although the process of folding the carrier over is likely to crease your clothes.

When you are going to be away for a long trip and need a large suitcase, for check-in be sure to select a large enough case with some flexibility. Hard cases are great but very unforgiving if you need to pack a few extra items into an already bulging case.

If you do have to check in your large case, find some unique way of identifying it so that you can spot it on the baggage carousel.

Packing and repacking

Our main rule for packing is to think very carefully about every single item you pack. Do not carry lots of unnecessary items.

The best way to ensure that you do not over or under pack is to sit down and carefully work out a schedule for your trip, whether it is business or pleasure. Work out the events you will be attending over the days you are away, formal, informal, dinners etc., and then ensure that you have the right clothes for each event.

Be sure to include shoes, belts, ties and any other items you may require and make sure that everything matches and is co-ordinated. One way to ensure that you have the maximum possible range of combinations is to stick to a limited colour palette. Dark suits, a range of jackets and trousers that are interchangeable, light shirts and a number of ties so that you do not repeat.

If it is a long trip you may well be able to get clothes cleaned or dry cleaned, but if you are rapidly moving from one place to another this may not be possible as a hotel usually requires 28 – 48 hours to turn round washing and dry cleaning.

Often you will be travelling to more than one location and this will require packing, unpacking and then repacking multiple times, so it is important to follow some basic rules to ensure everything arrives in a reasonable state.

Learn how to fold a suit or jacket properly and how to roll trousers to minimize creasing.

Folding a jacket can be one of the most difficult things to do, so here is the Perfect Gentleman's recommended method:

- Take each of the jacket sleeves and pull them inside out.

- Take the jacket by the middle of its collar in your left hand and with the back of the jacket towards you.

- Fold the jacket in half

- Place the left shoulder into the right shoulder. There should be a good fit.

- Put the left sleeve on top of the right sleeve and flatten the sleeves.

- Finally make sure that the jacket is as flat as possible.

- Fold the jacket into thirds from top to bottom and place carefully in your case.

- Fold your shirts in half at the collar and then roll them tightly to minimize creasing.

- If you are using a wheeled suitcase pack the heavy items at the bottom (wheeled) end of the suitcase to avoid them pressing down on lighter items.

- While you may not bother with pyjamas when you are at home it is always a wise idea to pack suitable night attire if you are staying in a hotel, thus avoiding the risk of having to search around your room for something to wear in the dark in the event of a fire alarm.

- When you arrive and unpack it is likely that suits, jackets, trousers and shirts will have become creased, even if you are an expert and experienced packer. To remove creases hang the items on coat hangers above a bath full of hot water and close the bathroom door. Over a couple of hours the steam will remove most of the wrinkles. Be sure to allow sufficient time for the clothes to dry out before you need to wear them.

- Many hotels will provide an iron and an ironing board either in the room or to be delivered to your room on request. You will however, need to know how to iron so be sure to practice before you go. Also be careful with the settings on the iron so that you do not ruin your favourite shirt. Always iron your suit through a slightly damp towel of cloth to avoid marking the suit or making the fabric shiny.

- If you have ever wondered why it is harder to close your case on the way back from a trip than it is time you started to look at the way you have packed your dirty items. The temptation to just throw them into a spare plastic bag or a plastic hotel laundry bag means that they will take up much more space than when carefully packed at the start of your trip, so pack your dirty items as carefully as you did when you started.

Wash kit & toiletries

When packing your wash bag for your trip there is always a compromise between weight and carrying enough to last the trip. It is always best to pack enough to last because you can never be certain to have the time to shop and it may not be possible to get your preferred brand in another country. With the recent restrictions on travelling with liquids in hand luggage it is likely that your wash kit will need to be packed in your main luggage.

If you are on a long flight you may decide that you need to clean your teeth before you disembark so it is a good idea to pack a small toothbrush and a tiny tube of toothpaste in your hand luggage. We do not recommend attempting to shave on a plane. There is insufficient space and with possible turbulence the risks are not worth it. Not to mention the look on the face of the gentleman or lady who has been waiting outside the toilet while you shaved.

Our recommended kit is as follows:

- Toothbrush and toothpaste
- Dental floss
- Mouthwash
- Razor and shaving cream
- Spare razor blades
- Shampoo and conditioner
- Hairbrush and / or comb

- Soap

- Deodorant

- Moisturiser

- Cologne

What to wear when travelling

Think carefully about the clothes you wear while travelling. Loose fitting, flexible clothing may be a description that fits a tracksuit, but a Travelling Gentleman should find suitable clothing in his wardrobe to be comfortable while travelling while still remaining stylish.

Dress smartly to travel. With today's sophisticated IT systems and loyalty programs it is less likely that you will be picked out of the check-in queue for an upgrade just because you are wearing a jacket and tie, but it cannot hurt.

Wear looser clothes and ideally ones that do not crease. Many hours of sitting in an aircraft seat with a seat belt on will put a stress on the look of most clothes.

Think carefully about your jacket. It is highly likely to be removed and, unless you are travelling business class, there is no likelihood of it being hung up, so it will need to be rolled up and put in the overhead bin for the duration of the flight so we recommend that you do not select your finest suit for travelling.

Consider the temperature on board a plane and wear layers, which are easy to put on and take off if you feel too cold or too hot.

Always wear socks when travelling. This may sound obvious but if you are on the way to or from holiday you may well decide to do without. But cold air circulates around the floors of a plane in a most unpleasant way.

Wear comfortable footwear, ideally slip-ons. It is great to be able to slip your shoes off and relax. However, do remember that while in a pressurised plane your feet will swell, so if you take your shoes off make sure they are flexible enough to get back on if your feet swell slightly.

We recommend travelling in dark colours. Eating and drinking in a confined space is not easy and arriving in a foreign country with coffee stains on a pair of cream chinos does not create the right impression.

If you are travelling from the UK or to a colder country you may well need a coat for travelling to and from the airport. Select a lightweight rainproof jacket that will fit easily into the outer pocket of your suitcase. That way you can slip it off when you arrive at the airport and pack it away for the journey, and it will be quickly accessible when you arrive.

Research the likely climate of the country you are travelling to and make sure that you go prepared. Travelling to New York in January with clothes suitable for a UK spring is likely to leave you needing a trip to the shops to buy a heavy coat, hat and gloves.

Technology

Today any Gentleman Traveller is likely to have a wealth of technology in his bag or briefcase. With access to the Internet, a huge array of travel apps, and websites offering advice and customer feedback, there is no shortage of information available for the traveller however remote the place to which you are travelling.

Consider useful travel apps that may be available:

- Apps from either your airport or airline to advise you on any delays or issues with your flight.

- Local guides or recommendations for restaurants

- Be sure that you clearly understand the costs of using your mobile phone in the country that you are travelling to. Talk to your provider and explore the possibility of a travel 'bundle' to allow you to make cheaper calls.

- The rates for data usage in most overseas countries are prohibitive. In most cases the best policy is to switch your data service off when you leave the UK and leave it off when you are travelling to avoid nasty surprises on your bill when you return.

- It is also worth exploring the possibility of using a 'travel sim' for your phone when you are away. These work with a new number (which you can give to your key contacts) and usually offer a much-reduced tariff.

- Ensure that you pack all the required cables, chargers, memory cards and disk drives for your phones, tablets and cameras.

- You will also need sufficient travel adapters for your electrical devices. An alternative to buying lots of travel adapters it to take just one travel adapter and a four way adapter or a plug strip with four sockets.

Airline loyalty schemes

If you are a frequent traveller and a regular user of one or two airlines there are many perks available to you through airlines' frequent flyer schemes. These are likely to include air miles, the opportunity to select your seat on line before others and, most important for the frequent flyer, the opportunity to get an upgrade.

Always join the schemes of the airlines you use and use their online systems to make your booking. This will ensure your booking is linked to your account and will maximize your frequent flyer points.

If you are a frequent business flyer and can decide which airline to fly on, be sure to read and understand the rules. If you have flown many hours with an airline you should ensure that you can benefit from some free or discounted travel for your leisure time as a perk.

Check-in

As airlines improve their technology and look to cut costs the increased use of self-service check-ins can save you a lot of time in a queue. Read up about this on your airline's web site. Ensure you know how to use the system and what documents you need to print out before you travel.

Security

Always lock your suitcases wherever you are travelling, you might have to use approved locks when traveling to certain countries, and if you are particularly worried consider having your cases security wrapped.

Be aware that when carrying a laptop in your hand luggage it must go through the security scanner separately. To avoid delays be prepared for this and have it ready as you approach the scanner.

Airline Lounges

International travel, whether for business or for pleasure is never as glamorous as it appears. It can involve many hours sitting in airports waiting to board delayed flights or waiting for connections. Having access to a pleasant and well-equipped lounge can make delays more pleasant and much more comfortable.

If you are lucky enough to fly business class you will usually have access to a lounge prior to departure. These are usually quiet, free from screaming children. Hot drinks and light food are available and, in most cases free Wi-Fi, if you need to catch up on emails or do some work.

If you are a frequent economy class traveller it is worth looking at the Priority Pass card, which give you access to lounges all over the world. In many cases this, along with free travel insurance, may be included as part of an enhanced bank account. It is worth checking with your bank to see if they offer this benefit; it can be very cost effective if you are a frequent traveller.

Etiquette on board a plane

The Perfect Gentleman traveller can find his patience severely tested in the confines of a plane on a long flight.

Decide whether you prefer a window or aisle seat. This will usually be stored on the airline's systems if you are a loyalty card member.

Do not wrestle your neighbour for the armrest, you are going to be sitting together for a long time.

When you need to get up, push yourself out of your seat using the arm rests rather than pulling on the chair in front and disturbing another passenger.

Be considerate with headphones and do not have them too loud if you are in close proximity to another traveller.

If you have an issue with another traveller or a group of travellers take this up with the flight attendant. They are trained to handle these situations. Do not take matters into your own hands.

Health tips when flying

It is recommended that you consider various issues when travelling on an airplane, whether it is for a short or a long flight. Taking notice of these points will mean that you arrive in far better condition. This is particularly important if you have to go straight from the airport into important meetings.

Flying in a sealed environment where air is regularly re-circulated can mean that you share all the bugs that your fellow passengers may have. Using 'First Defense' nasal spray before you board the plane, and again during a long flight, can help to protect you from some of the airborne bugs.

Keep hydrated; the pressurised system is very drying, so sip water or orange juice often on the flight.

Avoid large amounts of alcohol and coffee before and during the flight. This will just have the effect of further dehydrating you.

On a long flight get up and walk about to stretch your legs, improve your blood circulation and to reduce the likelihood of other conditions.

Tips when flying Discount Airlines

You may be required, either by virtue of the route or company policy, to fly with one of the discount airlines and there are some tips which can make flying with these airlines more pleasant.

Paying extra to board a plane first if they have unreserved seating can be a waste of money if you are going to access the plane by a bus, as the first people onto the bus are usually the last ones onto the plane.

If you are flying alone it is often better to avoid the unseemly scrum at the gate as everyone jostles to get onto the plane. Wait in the lounge with your tea and your paper until everyone else has boarded the plane and then get on. It is highly likely that there will be one seat free in one of the first five rows which ensures you will be one of the first off the plane. These airlines make a large part of their revenue from the various extras that you have to buy from them onboard. Unless you particularly like Pringles or highly expensive sandwiches with wilting lettuce, consider buying food before you board. If you purchase food airside you will also be allowed to buy cold drinks to take onto the plane.

Paperwork

With the increase in computerised systems, online check-in and the booking of trips on the Internet, the responsibility for much of the travel documentation to get you safely to your destination will fall to you. So it is critical that you have everything that you need and that you have it organised in a folder where it is easy to find at the airport and when you arrive at your destination.

Be sure to print out any e-tickets and boarding passes required for your outward journey and possibly for your return journey.

Be sure to double check that you have completed all the information required by the Airlines online system. Due to security requirements in many countries it is necessary to provide a lot of details online prior to travelling and the responsibility to enter all this data is usually yours.

When you book your travel always check that you can locate your passport and that it is valid for the whole period of your trip and ideally a few months beyond. If your passport needs to be renewed check online to ensure that you have enough time to get a new passport back by the time you travel and do this **BEFORE** you book your trip.

Double-check the requirements for visas in the country that you are travelling to. If in doubt, your Travel Company or airline should be able to advise you.

Ensure that you have all the vouchers you require for hotels if you have pre-booked them through a holiday company.

Make sure that you have vouchers for airport transfers.

Always double check your hotel booking(s) before you travel and always carry a copy of the booking with you to avoid any possible confusion.

Make sure to check carefully that the dates of arrival and departure are correct and that any special requests have been included on the booking form.

Health

Being ill while you are travelling can ruin a trip. Make sure you take all possible precautions and carry with you a basic kit of medicines to cover the most likely issues.

Be sure to check whether you need any specific injections or medication for the area you are travelling to.

Carry a basic health and first aid kit with you and check it before each trip. Buying the right medication overseas can be expensive;

you may not be able to get the brand you want and spending time chasing around for a chemist in the middle of the night because you forgot something can really ruin your day.

Our recommended travel health kit includes:

- Personal prescribed medication (ensure you have enough for your full trip and a little to spare)

- Pain control – Aspirin or Paracetemol unless you are used to something stronger.

- A good diarrhea medicine such as Diocalm or Imodium

- Rehydrating salt sachets to aid rehydration in the event of stomach upsets

- A good sunscreen and a sun hat

- Any medication for allergies – antihistamines, etc.

- Plasters for minor cuts

- Antibiotic ointment to help with minor scrapes and cuts

When you arrive...

Hotels

Your hotel room is your home away from home. If you are a frequent traveller there are various ways that you can personalise even the most sterile room and make it feel like home including taking your own music, small pictures from home and even candles or room fragrance to create an atmosphere of familiarity. Be sure to check the situation on smoke detectors before you use a candle though!

If you land very early and need a room to change and freshen up before an important meeting, be sure to specify this and double-check that it will be available.

Hotels, like airlines have loyalty schemes these days and it is well worth joining them if you are a frequent traveller. Once you have been recognised by the system as a good customer you will be considered for upgrades and will be given free nights stay.

Security

While your technology may be commonplace at home it can be exotic and expensive in foreign countries and thus a key target for criminals, so you need to be cautious when using technology in public places. Phone companies also make huge profits from travellers, so be very aware of how your systems are set up when travelling. It is best to turn off "data roaming" on your phone while abroad.

If you carry lots of electronic devices you will be a target for thieves. Today's mobile phones and tablet computers are highly sought after gadgets all around the world.

Do not leave your expensive gadgets, your passport, credit cards and your wallet out in the open, either in your hotel room or when you are out and about.

Do not put temptation in people's way. Pulling out a stuffed wallet, a top of the range phone, your iPad or a brand new iPhone in an area crowded with strangers can mark you out as a target for criminals.

Always rent a safe in your hotel, either in the room or reception. Lock up your valuable items and keep the safe locked at all times except when you need them.

Be sure that you are aware of your security. Think about where you carry your wallet and passport. If necessary, wear trousers with a zip pocket or a money belt for safety.

Be aware that thieves can take items out of your bag if you are not vigilant. Backpacks are particularly susceptible, so consider one with a double zip and put a padlock on it. The extra few seconds it takes to unlock it will be worth it. Going to the police to report an item stolen (often a requirement of travel insurance) will take hours of your valuable time.

Ensure that you only take with you credit and debit cards, which you can use in the country to which you are travelling. Only take the cards you need and be sure to go through your wallet before you leave and remove any cards that you will not need while travelling (store cards, membership cards etc.)

Having made doubly sure that you have backed up all your phone data, you now need to be sure that your phone is secure. Make sure that you have a pin lock on the phone so that in the event that you lose it or it is stolen you will not be presented with a huge bill on your return.

Data security – always back up all your electronic devices before you travel. This includes lap-tops, tablets, phones and cameras. Hardware can be replaced, usually under insurance, but replacing your data, phone numbers, apps and important photographs is impossible if you have not backed up your data.

Insurance

In some countries having travel insurance is mandatory. It is possible to get single trip insurance on an annual policy if you are a frequent traveller.

Always ensure that you have suitable travel insurance. Be sure you have read at least the headline details of the policy and always travel with the policy so you know what to do if you need to make a claim.

Many private bank accounts will include travel insurance as part of a package of benefits to their customers and this is worth investigating and working out the costs (you will typically have to pay a charge for using these accounts).

Drinking

Make sure that (as would be expected of a Perfect Gentleman in any city) you maintain control.

Do not drink too much and do not get lured into bars you do not know.

Guidebooks

Do not just go for the mainstream guidebooks or you will just end up where everyone else eats. Pick the smaller guides, follow a blogger whose suggestions you trust, or check out places on Trip Advisor.

In our experience the best eating experiences we have had were in restaurants where the locals eat rather than in large expensive restaurants, which are a trap for tourists and their money. In small local places the food is better quality, better priced and the ambiance is better because they are full of locals rather than fellow tourists.

Tipping

To avoid any 'misunderstandings' it is important to understand the local expectations for tipping in bars and restaurants.

In many countries where there is no minimum wage a large part of a waiter's pay may be made up of tips. While this often results in a great improvement in the quality of the service it can lead to some issues if the service has been good and you have failed to understand the local customs and leave insufficient tip. In a famous steak restaurant in Chicago a Gentleman was very nearly marched out of the establishment by his collar by a very large and angry waiter somewhat disappointed at being left a 10% tip when the local expectation was around 20%.

If your housekeeper at your hotel has done a good job, be sure to leave something for her in your room when you leave. In many countries tips are the main source of wages, so think about this when tipping.

Romance

Holiday or business trip romances can be a dicey thing, for many reasons. One being, it is highly likely that if a woman makes a beeline for you, even in some of the better hotels, she might have ulterior motives than just making your acquaintance.

Presents

All too often on business trips you will get wrapped up in meetings and dinners and before you know it you will be in the departure lounge on your way home. Make sure that your loved ones understand it is that type of trip or you will end up buying expensive gifts from a very limited range in the departure lounge.

Alternatively, be sure to allocate sufficient time to go shopping to buy something that shows your loved ones that you were thinking of them while you were away.

Behaviour and safety

Being a Perfect Travelling Gentleman is an opportunity to demonstrate to the rest of the world that you are a Gentleman.

Do not be loud or aggressive. Try to blend in and you will be able to go to places and see things that the majority of travellers do not see.

Prolonged eye contact can be seen as an aggressive stance in some countries, so be careful until you understand the local customs and ways.

Be cautious and develop a "radar" for your own safety. Do not go into areas in which you do not feel safe.

Avoid standing around looking at a map, it immediately marks you out as a tourist and, for some people, a target.

General

Travelling the world has never been easier. The Travelling Gentleman should be able to move comfortably and stylishly around the world. Travelling can be a huge pleasure, you will see amazing things, broaden your education, develop your understanding of the way the world works and meet new and interesting people.

Take your time, and enjoy your surroundings. Be adventurous while at the same time being safe. Find out where the locals go and do not just accept either the places set up for tourists or the same multinational brands that you can get at home.

The Travelling Gentleman always returns from an overseas trip better educated and more aware both of himself and of the world around him.

Travel Checklist

We have put together this checklist to ensure your trip goes smoothly.

Please modify it and make it your own.

Item	
Luggage	
Suitcase	
Carry on case	
Padlocks for all cases	
Clothes	
Pyjamas	
Suits	
Jackets	
Trousers	
Shirts – working	
Shirts - casual	
Ties	
Belts	
Shoes	
Underwear	
Socks	
Swimming trunks	

Gym kit	
Trainers	
Rain Coat	
Wash Kit	
Toothbrush and toothpaste	
Dental floss	
Mouthwash	
Razor and shaving cream	
Spare razor blades	
Shampoo and conditioner	
Hairbrush and / or comb	
Soap	
Deodorant	
Moisturiser	
Cologne	
Razor and shaving cream	
Spare razor blades	
Shampoo and conditioner	
Hairbrush and / or comb	
Soap	
Deodorant	
Cards and documents	
Credit cards	
Debit cards	
Airport lounge card	
Passport	

Visa paperwork	
Tickets	
Boarding card	
Hotel vouchers	
Airport transfer vouchers	
Copy of your travel insurance policy	
Guide books	
Technology	
Mobile phone	
Mobile phone charger	
Plug converter	
Laptop	
Tablet	
Camera	
Camera charger or batteries	
Memory cards	
iPod	
iPod charger	
Headphones	
Alarm clock	
Health	
First defence spray	
First Aid kit	
Personal prescribed medication (ensure you have enough for your full trip and a little to spare)	

Pain control – Aspirin or Paracetemol, unless you are used to something stronger.	
A good diarrhoea medicine such as Diocalm or Imodium	
Rehydrating salt sachets to aid rehydration in the event of stomach upsets	
A good sunscreen (and make sure you also have a sun hat)	
Any medication for allergies – antihistamines etc	
Plasters for minor cuts	
Antibiotic ointment to help with minor scrapes and cuts	

THE BRIEF GENTLEMAN'S CITY TRAVEL GUIDE

" I have wandered all my life, and I have also traveled; the difference between the two being this, that we wander for distraction, but we travel for fulfilment.

Hilaire Belloc

A Gentleman should travel and broaden his mind. In the previous chapter we have handed out some top advice for how to travel like a Perfect Gentleman, so in this chapter we will hopefully inspire you with some places to travel to, or indeed return to.

Therefore, here are our Ten Cities to visit and what to do while you are there:

Paris

Why go?

Paris is one of the smaller capital cities and a perfect size to walk around and discover, so take a sensible pair of comfortable walking shoes. But do not rush everywhere, take some time to sit, drink coffee and watch the world go by. There are a huge number of wonderful restaurants, art galleries, and shops not to mention all the iconic buildings and vistas.

When to go?

Spring (as the song says, it is the season to go!)

Autumn

Avoid August. In Paris almost everyone still manages to go away for the whole of the month, so many small and interesting shops and restaurants are likely to be closed or have only a minimum staff.

Where to Stay?

There are some amazing hotels in Paris, the George V is probably one of the finest hotels in the world and certainly one of the most famous, but when you have visited Paris you will realise that you spend very little time in your hotel room. It becomes somewhere to sleep and shower and very little else, so in our opinion there is very little reason to invest a huge amount in a sprauncy hotel room.

Flat rental is best. Search the web (sites like airbnb.com) for Paris flats to rent by the week or day, there are many available whether you are just two people or a bigger party. You will very quickly feel like you are a local once you have found your local bakery and coffee shop for breakfasts.

A Tiny hotel, there are a multitude of charming small hotels which offer you the minimum you will need i.e. a bed and a shower. Most will offer you the option of breakfast, often on a tray left outside your door, with bread jam and coffee or hot chocolate, enough to get you up and going for the day. We suggest the Hotel de Notre Dame "Maitre Albert" a tiny hotel with a great location.

Top 5 things to do?

The Eiffel Tower - You will have to queue, it is one of Paris's main attractions after all, but you will be rewarded with amazing views over the city.

The Louvre - We recommend going as early as possible and doing the obvious first. Do not let it bother you if it is a huge scrum, the French do not do orderly queuing. Then take as much time as you can spare wandering the wondrous galleries. Make sure you go down into the basements to see some of the original foundations of Paris.

The Musee Dorsee - This converted station houses a wonderful museum of modern art.

Walk around the back streets of Le Marais and/or St Germain where you will discover many delightful small shops including some wonderful chocolate shops, you might need an energy boost.

Sit in a Cafe and watch the world go by, it is what the Parisians love to do. Get people watching with a Café and a patisserie.

Some extras: the Rodin Museum, Notre Damme Cathedral, and the Sacre Ceour Church, to name but a few.

Where to eat?

Cut off the main drags, where most of the restaurants are just tourist traps, and head into one of the smaller districts and find the small restaurants where the locals eat. Remember that the French love their food so a restaurant that serves poor food is likely to go out of business pretty quickly.

For a Bistro Experience try Le Bougainville tucked away in the chic Galerie Vivienne.

For Movie Buffs, Le Grand Colbert is from the film '*Something's Gotta Give*' and interesting to visit.

Rome

Why go?

The 'Eternal City' is a bustling buzzing place with modern life rushing around some of the relics of the ancient Roman civilization. There is nowhere like it. It is a city of history, religion and romance.

A huge central area of classical Rome sits in the middle of the modern city.

When to go?

Rome is a city full of tourists almost all year round, so do not expect peace and quiet. Instead, enjoy the hustle and bustle of the city, which is half the fun.

But April to June and September to October are best and August is generally a month to avoid.

Where to Stay?

Think carefully about your hotel, a central location is likely to be extremely expensive and possibly noisy, and some smaller cheaper hotels can leave you way out of the city. Find a smaller hotel tucked away but fairly central, if you are lucky it will have a rooftop restaurant where you can enjoy your breakfast looking out over the city with the promise of the day stretching before you. We suggest the Fortyseven Hotel or the delightful Hotel Raphael.

Once again use a website like www.airbnb.com to find a local flat as it will probably be more interesting.

Top 5 things to do?

Coliseum – naturally, you must.

Walk around fountains and the markets, they are inspiring and delicious!

Take a trip to The Catacombs.

The Vatican - the queues can be huge, but there are always people who can help you get in quicker, be careful which one you pick as some are just scammers. For many just a trip to St Peter's square can be sufficient.

Dress up and head for the Opera.

Where to eat?

Find small restaurants off the tourist path, and go early to be sure of getting a table.

Try a pizza at a local restaurant, there are many fabulous ones to try, local favourite Li Roni.

Dazzle your tastebuds with Gelato (Ice cream) – perhaps try Gelateria La Romana.

Coffee and cake, try *Sant'Eustachio.*

Be aware of pickpockets around the major tourist attractions. Think about the vulnerability of your bags and back packs, some of these professional thieves can be in and out of your back pack before you have missed anything.

Istanbul

Why go?

Istanbul sits half in Asia and half in Europe and this juxtaposition of cultures, together with its ancient roots and the fact that its state has remained steadfastly (non religious), the many cultural mixes have created a city unlike any other.

When to go?

Spring, this city has many beautiful gardens and in the cool of spring the beauty of the city is wonderful for the visitor.

Where to Stay?

Stay centrally on the European side of the city, there are many great central hotels. Perhaps the Hotel Sultania in the centre of town.

If it is a special trip consider the Pera Palace with its rickety old lifts and historic rooms, you will expect to find Agatha Christie or Hercule Poirot (fresh from a trip on the Orient Express) coming round the corner to greet you.

Top 5 things to do?

Blue Mosque (Sultan Ahmet Mosque) – The Inspiring building will send you back to ancient times.

Grand Bazaar and the Spice Bazaar – You will feel like a merchant with your haggling skills.

Hammam – The traditional Turkish Bath will leave you feeling invigorated.

Tea and a pipe – You must sample the local ways and people watching whilst sipping tea and nargileh, especially on an evening in Tophane.

Trip across the Bosphorous and see the spectacular city as thousands of travellers before you have done.

Where to eat?

The food in Istanbul can be magnificent despite the fact that many of the locals have decided that the height of international cuisine for the traveller is the jacket potato, and there are stalls everywhere.

We suggest Pandeli, near the Spice Bazaar or perhaps Hamdi Et Lokantasi or SuAda for the view.

Istanbul is a magical city and one of the great places to visit, especially for a Historical Gentleman.

London

Why go?

Even if you live in the UK you should always visit London regularly because it is such a vibrant and changing city, each area can be an adventure in itself.

When to go?

Any time of year because there is always something interesting going on but probably best to avoid the 'grey' months of January, February, March.

Where to Stay?

In the last 20 years London has moved towards the model of New York and is pretty much a city that never sleeps, except some of the transport infrastructure with tubes closing down relatively early. But with night busses and one of London's finest resources, the ever present black cabs, it is possible to get anywhere in central London for a few pounds and later at night when there is little or no traffic the fares can be very reasonable. Unless you are staying at peak time there are likely to be plenty of choices.

Top 5 things to do?

London Eye – The newest of London's Attractions and well worth the view on a good day.

Borough Market – One of London's funkiest food markets, full of good food and surrounded by restaurants. Remember to walk along the South Bank of the river Thames to get there.

St Paul's Cathedral – This great church is Sir Christopher Wren's masterpiece and still wows when surrounded by the gleaming towers of glass of the city. Grab a tour with one of the guides who are exceptionally knowledgeable.

Victoria & Albert Museum - One of London's unsung Museums as it is across the road from the grand Natural History Museum; full of different art and design wonders from all through history and around the world. Get lost in here.

There is so much to do and see in London, try to walk around London as much as possible. You will discover plenty.

Where to eat?

The days of the stereotypes of bad British food is long gone, the UK and Ireland received more Michelin Stars than the USA and Spain last year. London itself has sixty-five Michelin Stars and over fifty Bib Gourmands, and there are many other great restaurants too.

As with all places, if you stay away from the Tourist areas the prices get a little more reasonable. Here is a selection of some of our favorites.

Try Fish & Chips in the Golden Hind in Marylebone.

Grab a Sunday Roast at the Historic Spaniards Inn in Hampstead or, for classic British, head to Rules in Covent Garden.

Want Breakfast? Go to the stylish Riding House Café near Oxford Circus or slap up style at Terry's Café near Borough Market, or Beppe's near Smithfield Meat Market.

We are working on a Perfect Gentleman's Guide to London to fill out more details and help the intrepid traveller.

Chicago

Why go?

The' Windy city' has so much to offer with fantastic galleries, museums, restaurants, and, lest we forget...the blues.

When to go?

May to October, avoid the winter. It was originally called the 'windy city' because of its powerful politicians, but it is an apt name for the weather there too. There are not many places that have heated pavements (or sidewalks) because the temperature stays so low for so long.

Where to Stay?

Palmer House Hilton is nice and central.

The Drake is very up market and deco smart.

Top 5 things to do?

John Hancock Tower – Head to the top for fantastic views.

Wrigley Field – Probably the home of old style baseball!

The Art Institute of Chicago - A great collection of French impressionists and some amazing miniature rooms in the basement.

A Blues Club - there are so many to choose from, check local newspapers or websites for a guide.

Wicker Park - Take a walk in and absorb the neighbourhood.

Where to eat?

Chicago is my kind of town, as the Master has sung. It covers all and every food type you could possibly imagine as well as being the foundation of traditional American type fare. There are so many, from the high end to the old school diner, but it is know for its steak.

We recommend Gene and Georgetti, best place in the world for steak according to PG2.

Have breakfast in the Bongo Room.

Old School Italian at Sabatino's.

The Classic Diner experience at White Palace Grill.

Venice

Why go?

Probably the most romantic city in the world, but the Venetians know this. When you consider the methods of transport, everything (food, drink, building materials etc.) has to come in by boat and everything (including rubbish) has to be removed by boat, together with their reliance on the tourist industry, and you will understand why the Venetians, who after all have been making a living this way for many hundreds of years, charge accordingly.

When to go?

It is almost always going to be busy, but avoid February (Carnival) and the very height of summer when you cannot move for tourists in the most popular spots.

One time to consider is Christmas. Although some restaurants and shops will be closed, the city is very peaceful and mostly deserted by tourists, which makes the holiday period a magical time in which you will feel you almost have the city to yourself.

Where to Stay?

If you search, or if you have a good travel agent, you will be able to find a number of 'central apartment hotels'. These may include rooms in a number of buildings all located around a small reception and serviced by a small dining room, which serves breakfast. This solution to the issue of building large hotels in historic Venice is a typically inventive Venetian idea and it works very well. You can come and go as you please with modern access control and the rooms are serviced for you. It also allows you to find your own lunches and dinners as you explore.

Top 5 things to do?

The Fish Market - near the Rialto Bridge is a fascinating place to visit early in the morning. The hustle and bustle and the old building itself are timeless.

Walk the City - This may be a city built on water, but to get the best from it you will need a sensible pair of shoes, around every corner is a wonderful vista or a great little bar to stop in for a coffee or a Belini (the local delight of fizz and peach juice) so walk, walk and then walk some more.

Vapereto tour - When your feet are tired take this circular tour and jump on jump off to see some of the most remote areas of the city.

The Glass Factories - Depending on how much time you have, a boat trip out to the glass factories of Murano is a great way to spend a few hours. The craftsmanship is amazing and the salesmanship is every bit as good.

Ponte di Rialto – Just because you have too! And get there for dawn and make it a memorable experience as the sun rises and there is less of a crowd!

Where to eat?

For all the historic beauty and wonder contained on the islands of Venice the cuisine lags somewhere behind and the huge number of visitors means that there is a vast number of formulaic tourist restaurants charging crazy prices for very average food. Nothing is cheap in Venice, but for a genuine experience, good service and the chance to rub shoulders with gondoliers as they grab their lunch, go to the Trattoria all Rivetta in the Castello District

Singapore

Why go?

It is our first Asian city on this list and probably one of the first ones to visit. It has been called variously 'Asia for beginners' or 'Switzerland in the Tropics'. It is a dynamic city that mixes multiple cultures all under one roof. It does not have the craziness, the history or the bustle of other cities in Asia, but it has something that makes it fascinating.

When to go?

With this city you can go anytime. The weather is exceptionally constant and fairly humid, but the temperature never really drops below 20C (68) with frequent rainstorms that usually blow away quickly.

It gets busy at certain times such as Chinese New Year and during the Formula 1 Grand Prix, but it always seems to work.

Where to Stay?

The City is full of hotels from business staples to luxury palaces to boutique gems. The main city is not that large so you can get around quite easily with a short taxi ride.

For the quintessential colonial experience you have to stay at The Raffles Hotel or for modern style try the Fullerton or the Shangri-La. For quirky, try either The Forest or The New Majestic, but our personal favourite is The Scarlet Hotel.

Top 5 things to do?

Shop on Orchard Road – The Singaporeans love to Shop and at over 2 km long this street caters for everything you could possibly imagine. You do not even have to get sweaty walking along the street as it is interconnected by more shopping malls.

Marina Bay – walk around the newly constructed bay area, where a great deal of the land has been reclaimed from the sea, and end up at the Marina Sands and their Skypark for a great view with a cocktail in hand.

Chinatown and Temples – The historical part of town away from the gleaming sky-scrappers.

The Night Safari at the Singapore Zoo – need we say more?!

A Singapore Sling at the Long Bar in the Raffles Hotel – We know it is clichéd, but it is worth the experience.

Where to eat?

Apart form shopping, the Number One thing they like to do is eat! So the amount of restaurants and cuisines here is phenomenal. Sunday Brunch in Singapore is a big thing and you might need to book for certain restaurants.

Mezza9 is great for a broad range of cuisine, try Dim Sum in Chinatown at Yum Cha. Try Samy's Curry in the old army barracks on Dempsey Hill and try the Maxwell Road Hawker centre.

San Francisco

Why go?

San Francisco is one of the most fascinating cities in the world; the richly diverse people who have found their way to the 'city on the bay' make it a fascinating and wonderfully stimulating city to spend time exploring. To top it all off, it is only a short car ride to the vineyards of California!

When to go?

Natives of the town say that the best months are September and October, also May is not too shabby. As a major city there is always something going on, so you can go at anytime.

Where to Stay?

Like any major city there is plenty on all levels and for all budgets. Try airbnb.com to find some interesting places.

The Harbour Court Hotel

A great hotel on Embarcadero with great rooms, some with amazing views over the bay and the Golden Gate Bridge.

The San Remo Hotel (Budget)

A beautiful hotel with compact rooms, which previously served as lodgings for local dockworkers. Try to get a room overlooking Mason Street or go the whole hog and take the Penthouse.

Top 5 things to do?

Ride the Cable Car - It is traditional but excellent, one of the best value rides is to grab a traditional Cable car and ride through the city. Great for fantastic views and a feeling of genuine history, we like the one that heads up at the amazing Nob Hill.

Fisherman's Wharf - It is touristy and busy, but you can walk along the wharfs, do some people watching, then take a walk along the sea front to the Presidio and see the Golden Gate Bridge.

Alcatraz – You have to go, it is one of those Bucket List things to do. Book as soon as you know you are heading there otherwise you might not get a seat, this is especially true for the great Night Tour.

Take a Trip to Sausalito – Take a ferry across to the lovely area across the bay, great views, good food and just peacefully lovely.

Castro & Haight-Ashbury – Two areas that have historical significance to this city and worth the walk around.

Before you go, read some Armistead Maupin (Tales of the City).

Where to eat?

Another city with a diverse restaurant pile to choose from, with a focus on fish and Chinese, it is a gastronomic experience you will enjoy.

Breakfast at The Lighthouse, whether you cycle across the bridge (as many do on a weekend) or take a bus, make sure you head over to the tranquility of Sausalito and this wonderful spot. Do not be put off if there is a queue, it is worth the wait.

Caffe Trieste, a great cafe that is an institution. Once a haunt of Kerouac it is loaded with history.

Book a table at Scoma's. It is a classic seafood institution.

Havana

Why go?

Havana is a city like no other. Its spirit and soul and the great Cuban people will leave you feeling energized unlike any other city you will visit. Much of the cities infrastructure was built at a time when Havana was the playground of rich Americans seeking a sunny hideaway from the more restrictive American regime at a time of prohibition. Today, over fifty years after the revolution which cut the country off from its near neighbours, the country is very poor in financial terms and many of its buildings are crumbling. But the climate, and the Cubans who remain, make it an exciting and vibrant city that feels like it is stuck in a time warp. This situation cannot last forever, so if you have the chance go now before everything changes, and not necessarily for the better!

When to go?

Go from November (once the hurricane season is over) to May before it gets too hot and humid in the Cuban summer. We suggest avoiding parts of February when the Habanos festival is on, as it becomes exceptionally busy.

Where to Stay?

There are a few very good modern (foreign owned) hotels in Havana and there are also many older hotels that can be extremely run down, so chose carefully. Check out the latest recommendations on your favourite holiday web site, the Nacional is famous but a little tired, perhaps try the Saratoga.

Alternatively, stay in one of the many Private Houses that cater for visitors. These Casa Paticulares are all Government licensed and will usually have a private entrance, living room and bathroom for you to use. It is also likely that you will get a far better breakfast than you get in any but the very best hotels.

Top 5 things to do?

Visit a cigar factory - Whether you enjoy a fine Havana cigar or not, seeing the amazing process where a series of leaves are transformed into a beautiful cigar is similar to visiting a champagne house in Rheims, not to be missed.

Walk around the old city (Havana Vieccha) - In recent years the Cuban Government has realised the power of the tourist euro or pound and has invested hugely in renovating and preserving the heart of the old city of Havana and some of its beautiful buildings. If you can, go early in the morning before the tours start.

Go to a Cuban Night club - You are never far away from music anywhere in Havana, but a visit to a nightclub is a must. Our advice is to avoid some of the big names, which are little more than tourist joints, and head for something really authentic. The finest of these is Gato Tuerto (the one eyed cat) where you can rub shoulders with the locals and enjoy some wonderful entertainment until the small hours.

Take a tour of the city in a classic old American open top car - Back in the day all of the streets were full of big American cars (usually with Russian mechanicals under the 'hood') and somehow many of them are still to be found in Havana. A tour in an open top 1950's car should take a couple of hours and cover all the major sites. Be clear on the fee and the timing up front as two hours can get stretched to three and your bill will stretch too.

Drink a Mojito and smoke a cigar on the Terrace of the Nacional Hotel - The Hotel Nacional was built in the 1950's and is now a national monument. It is a great place to stay for a couple of nights, or just to visit for an evening to enjoy a Mojito and possibly a cigar on its huge horse shoe-shaped, covered terrace overlooking the entrance to Havana's harbour. Be sure to visit the Historic bar area where pictures of many of the hotel's famous visitors adorn the walls.

Where to eat?

If you have friends or acquaintances who have been to Cuba, there is a very good chance that they will have returned with tales of dreadful food from the major hotels. It is also possible to eat at some wonderful privately run restaurants and 'Paladars' where you will find food every bit as good as any top London restaurant but with a wonderful Cuban flavour.

The most famous of these is La Guarida. Made famous as the setting of a famous Spanish art house movie, it is a small family residence on the third floor of what looks from street level like a condemned building that has been turned into Havana's most famous restaurant, where even the queen of Spain has eaten. You will have to book and it is strongly recommended that you take a taxi to get there, but your efforts will be rewarded with a memorable lunch or dinner.

Many new small Paladars are springing up all over Havana as restrictions are taken off private enterprise. To find out the best places to eat and the best spots for music we recommend you look up www.havana-concierge.com This is a service run by a British expat who has lived in Havana for many years. You can use their English speaking service to help you book places to eat as well as organising all kinds of tours and trips.

One last thing, we have not forgotten that manners and etiquette differ around the globe and either through our magazine The Code of the Gentleman (www.codeofthegentleman.com) or in a future Perfect Gentleman book we will address these interesting issues.

THE ROMANTIC GENTLEMAN

" The word 'romance,' according to the dictionary, means excitement, adventure, and something extremely real. Romance should last a lifetime."

Billy Graham

The Lost Art of Wooing

" A heaven on earth I have won by wooing thee."

All's Well That Ends Well, William Shakespeare

At the Perfect Gentleman, we believe that it seems we have lost the art of romance, of wooing. It is like the Gentleman himself; hundreds of years of history pushed aside by the force of the modern world.

We do not believe that those early Homo Sapiens thought too much about what flowers to give nor how to approach a female of the species. The cartoon image of the pre-historic male clubbing the desired partner and dragging her back to his cave by hair abides in all our memory. The problem is for most men this is still not too far from the modern male approach. As with the Gentlemanly traits, we have forgotten how to romance someone. We are not tarring all men with the same brush and yet the brutish demeanour abounds throughout the current world and in some ways is still promoted.

These habits are rooted in the foundations of the practical nature of relationships. The reasons for ancient pair bonding were practical; it was about increasing the species. In ancient times Polygamy was normal, though not financially and practically possible and men could leave if the lady was infertile.

Good women were scarce in ancient times and therefore potential wives were literally captured. One tribe would raid another for females, not only to grab wives but to also increase the diversity of the children that would be born. This then turned into a custom in some areas of the world, where the Men would come into the village to 'steal' their potential brides. It is a custom that can still be seen in a different form today with the Romany or 'gypsy' people.

Wives, Partners and marriage became more and more a political and social standing tool as time progressed, not just about the bearing of children. Whether that was to forge alliances between families, securing a lineage of healthy children or in some cases even as blackmail. It was not always the case that the partnership was for these reasons, there were love matches but they were seen as the exception and not the rule, a great many marriages were arranged.

Love and Romance were not always left out of the equation. The ancient Greeks and Romans wrote eloquently on Love, they even had four different words for Love. Plato wrote that "love was the joy of the good, the wonder of the wise, the amazement of the gods'. Many tales of the gods from Ancient Greece were about love, lust and the power of love to conquer or cause harm. One of the most famous is that of the siege of Troy, an extensive war started over one woman, Helen, and the love that men bore her, she was the 'face that launched a thousand ships'. This was the exception and not the rule.

Christianity changed the wooing playing field from the 6th to 9th centuries in which marriage was formalized alongside the rise and establishment of the feudal system. These two factors, it has been hypothesized, brought about the ideals of 'Courtly Love', upon which almost all modern romantic traditions are based.

Courtly Love

Joyous in love, I make my aim
forever deeper in Joy to be.
The perfect Joy's the goal for me:
so the most perfect lady I claim.

Guilhem IX of Poitou aka William of Aquitaine (1071-1126)

The Troubadours of France started telling tales of courtly love. This medieval concept was about bringing nobleness and romance to the relations between men and women, especially among the nobility.

It was brought to the English Court by Eleanor of Aquitaine, her Grandfather (the poet from the quote above) being the first known troubadour poet.

The factors that influence Courtly Love are the same basis for romance for the Modern Gentleman. Its roots are based in the Crusades, as William of Aquitaine was on the first Crusade and involved with Spain and its Arabic influences. The Arabic poets were already expressing similar overtures of love. The second Influence was that of the feudal world and the fact that there was a need to control the lustful young knights in the service of their Lord. Showing them the way to behave towards the Lady of the land and the Ladies of Court. The Ideas of Courtly Love were popularized by the authors of the time, such as our friend Geoffrey Chaucer in The Canterbury Tales.

The rules of Courtly Love are derived from the Troubadours tales and the Latin poet Ovid's 'Ars Amatoria'. It was codified in Andreas Capellanus's 'De Amore', and, although there is some suggestion that this was a satirical work, it gives an indication of the things that were thought about, such as:

No one should be deprived of love without the very best of reasons

Every act of a lover ends in the thought of his beloved

Good character alone makes any man worthy of love

Courtly Love was not really about marital bliss, but instead was the start of developing the art of wooing.

Let Wooing Commence

The motto of chivalry is also the motto of wisdom; to serve all, but love only one.

Honore de Balzac

The code of Chivalry, as we discussed in other chapters, is linked with the principles of courtly love. If Courtly Love was part of the ideology, especially with reference to the duties to women, then

Chivalry was the practical application of that belief. This aspect of Chivalry is the one we are most familiar with today. The three aspects of Chivalric Love were; Romantic Deeds, Gallantry and Vassalage. All of these have lasted into modernity in one way or another.

The Romantic Deeds of old were the writing of poetry, the composing of ballads, and the giving of tokens. These are still an effective part of today's wooing strategy as they were then.

Gallantry refers to heroic, courageous and noble behaviour as well as polite and courteous attention to women, which also indicates that not only were men expected to behave correctly, they were also supposed to perform heroic deeds for the objects of their affection. This is as true today as it was then.

The concept of vassalage is probably the one most distant from today's world, but it plays a traditional and important part in today's courting rituals. The 'vassal' was the feudal term, which meant a person who entered into a dependent relationship with a Lord or Monarch. The obligations could include military service and work from the dependent and the lord would provide protection and perhaps lands and titles. What does that have to do with modern wooing? It has two great influences, the first being that the dependent would pledge his faith to the lord and in today's world this would be similar to the declarations of love and promises of faith and fidelity that men make to women. The second is more visual, the vassal would kneel on one knee to his Lord, and we can see this in the tradition of getting down on one knee to propose to your future bride.

The practices of wooing began with the knights of medieval Europe and have worked their magic like Merlin in the Arthurian Legend through the centuries till today.

What do Women Want?

If you know what women want, you can rule!

J M Perkins (Bette Midler) – What Women Want (2000)

If we fully knew the answer to this question, we would have bottled it and sold it already. There are piles of books, thousands of articles and a great many experts out there that are there to help you guide the seas of love, many of which are excellent and some of which are simply not.

So why should we throw our hat, though it is a snazzy one, into this crowded ring? We at the Perfect Gentleman believe that there is a simple and gentlemanly way to romance, to regain the wooing ground and bring back some key principles. We know that each person and each situation is different as we are all the White Knight in our own romance tale, but hopefully we can provide some interesting insights and some key tips. So what do women want?

Respect

It is one of our founding principles and it is the founding principle in the building blocks of relationships. Demonstrate that you respect the lady's opinions, career, hobbies, minds and their bodies.

Romance

The little acts of love; buying flowers, writing love notes, lighting candles, kissing and so much more. Do not forget to use them all the time, not just at the beginning of a relationship.

Time

Time is probably the most precious commodity in today's world, so remember to treat the person you love as the top priority. Spend time with them, even if it is just doing the washing up and talking.

Communication

The ability to communicate is key. Communication is not talking; communication is the ability to be understood. So make sure that you listen to what is being said and also seek to be understood, a grunt just will not do.

Passion & Ambition

Passionate and Ambitious people are infectious; people will be drawn to them as friends, work colleagues and lovers. Be passionate about who you are and be ambitious about what you can achieve.

Confidence

In most surveys this generally comes top of what most people find attractive. Confidence in yourself is key and can be built, as we have mentioned earlier.

Humour

This is always on every list of things that women look for. We are not expecting you to be a stand-up comedian, but a good sense of humour and the ability to make people laugh, even at yourself, will go a long way.

These are just the key principles to helping you become that Romantic Gentleman. You should take them to heart and develop them. We are here to help you, so let's start at the beginning.

An Approach

You had me at "hello".

Dorothy (Renée Zellweger), Jerry Maguire (1996)

One of the most daunting aspects of any relationship is the initial encounter from the daring of approaching someone in a bar to the relative safety of being introduced to someone at a party of friends. The initial contact plays a crucial part in your romantic journey.

Get the Look

First things first, how you look is important, so make sure that you have taken care of that element. We have already discussed in the previous chapters with tips for style, dress and grooming. Remember first impressions count.

Right Time, Right Place

Make sure the situation is appropriate. It might not be best to talk to a work colleague in front of everyone nor approach a waitress while she is working.

Just Say Hello

No cheesy chat up lines and no strategy from 'The Game'. Just walk up and say hello, in a quietly confident and calm manner. Start a conversation; make it about a shared point, whether that's the coffee, the music, a book or something in the News (good news only). Introduce yourself and then listen. If you have a point of introduction from someone else then your job is easier. This is the hardest part.

The Eyes Have It

Eye Contact is key. The right level of eye contact is crucial, you do not want to come across as a glaring mad man nor do you want to be a catching every movement. It is said that about 7 seconds of direct eye contact is comfortable. You do want to know what colour eyes she has at the end of the conversation.

Do not Fence Me In

Physical presence is important, our body language and positioning is key. Be non-threatening, be calm and do not back the lady into a corner or trap her in anyway, she will want an escape route. It does matter if you are not as physically imposing as Arnold Schwarzenegger, but you are still a male and there is always a possibility you are not a gentleman in their mind.

Listen, Listen, Listen

Make sure that they have heard you first and then ask a couple of questions and actively listen to the responses, not only will it give you the opportunity for continued conversation but will highlight the way the initial encounter is going.

Should I Stay or Should I Go?

Unless it is exceptionally obvious, for example she has walked away or you have immediately gone for a coffee, then you need to make a judgment call. Put simply, if she is maintaining eye contact and is pleasant and conversational then ask the lady out, if she is short with you and looking around then excuse yourself and move on.

Talking to someone for the first time is daunting, but a gentleman should challenge himself and be able to face his fears. Remember that Courage is one of the values of the Gentleman.

Online Dating

This is something the Gentleman of yesteryear never would have done, but times have changed and he moves with the times. Online Dating is now a respectable part of the dating landscape. As with everything in the world of the Internet, there is an infinite amount of possibilities and challenges as we navigate this new landscape.

Which Site?

You only have to 'google' online dating and you get dozens and dozens of sites each with different target audiences and kinds of profiles. Take time to peruse, look at the people on the site, both the potential partners and the male profiles to see whether you will fit in and attract the partners you are looking for.

The Profile

The best profiles are the gentle ones, the ones that are modest but clearly descriptive of themselves, the relationship sought and the ideal partner. The Hard Sell is equally off putting online as it is in the real world. If you are not the best wordsmith, read it out loud and see how it sounds.

The Picture

The single biggest male error is the photo. If the way you dress sets the first impression when you meet, the photo is the online equivalent. No 'Mug Shots', Selfies, nights out shots and no topless shots (even if you have the body of Adonis). Either have a professional one taken or get someone you know whom is good with a camera to do it. Make an effort and Smile!

1ˢᵗ Contact

When you find someone you like, the first email/phone call will make a very lasting impression. As with the face-to-face approach, discussed above, write with respect and care. No braggadocio, this is neither a CV nor a boasting competition. Show that you are a Gentleman from the start, mention items in their profile, especially mutual areas of interest. Be open and honest.

Moving On

If someone approaches you, take the time to do them the courtesy of engaging with them, you never know it might be your perfect match under a slightly different profile.

If you do move on, as any gentleman would, be polite, especially in your email to them. Also be a gentleman and accept rejection with an equal amount of good grace.

The Online principles of the Gentleman apply in the Romantic world as in every other aspect of you life.

The First Date

Always do something that requires you and your date to talk.

Steven Hill

You have made that daring step into the unknown and asked out someone you like so that you can spend time together and get to know each other better. Then the panic sets in, so breathe and let the team at the Perfect Gentleman guide you through our easy steps to have a great first date.

Firstly, what lies behind the date? The key elements are that you want to get to know each other better and show your very best side.

Taking that into consideration you want to go somewhere where it is easy to talk and interact. This is why one of the main reasons that a 'dinner date' is generally and most frequently a great first date. The key to a good first date is making it easy for everyone, especially the partner that you are taking out on the date, so think ahead. As with all Perfect Gentleman elements you have to prepare for the first date and try to take the possible headaches away.

Location, Location, Location

Where you are going and what you are doing is important, it sets a tone for the date and helps your date choose the clothing appropriately. Before you rush out and book your favourite Steak restaurant, check with your date that she is not a Vegetarian (which has happened to one of our Gentle Ladies).

Ask a few questions of the date, such as: What does she like to eat? And probably more importantly what she does not eat! Ask her what she likes to do. If you are not planning a Dinner Date you are going to need a few ideas on which to base your plans.

For first dates, we would avoid the following - Loud Music Concerts, Films and Theatre. After the first date these things come back into the mix, but as we said the first date is really about conversation not action. For outside of the box dates, think a walk, a museum, a picnic out (weather permitting) or a historical walk with a private guide and there are many others. The PG team have taken dates to Bookstores, the Zoo, the Planetarium, Wine Tastings and many more.

If you are choosing a restaurant, think about the food choices, simple and good is best, try and avoid messy food restaurants on the first date, you might think it is fun until your crisp white shirt is covered in some kind of sauce and you look like a slob.

Preferably choose a restaurant with No or very long turnaround times. You do not want to be in the middle of a great conversation when the Bill is placed in front of you!

If it is a dinner date, do let her know the restaurant, so she can look to dress appropriately. If you are doing something else, then do give your date the opportunity to be able to dress appropriately; you do not want her in High Heels if you are planning a walk through the park.

Finally, think about the impression you want to give of yourself, the date you choose will reflect that. Planning a walk round a Museum and then a casual lunch? Think about what message that conveys as does dinner at a very fancy restaurant that is generally out of your price bracket.

Think comfortable for you and the date. Think about your choice and make it relevant.

Clean, Style & Smooth

This is a date, it is about showing yourself off and therefore you should look your best.

Make sure you have showered, teeth brushed, shaved (for those with beards make sure it is clean and trimmed) and you are wearing a subtle fragrance. Please do not bathe in the fragrance, it is about subtlety. Oh and make sure the nails are clean and trimmed too!

As for style, dress appropriately to your date. We would always say dress one level higher than you think, as your date generally will. If it is dinner wear a suit and a good shirt, in more formal restaurants you should also wear a tie. If you are going out on your date during the weekend, perhaps wear a good pair of trousers, a shirt and a jacket. Please wear good shoes, not trainers as they make a stylish statement that you are no longer a boy.

Check out some of our style posts or Pintrest pages to get a few ideas for a stylish look.

Shhh Listen First

The art to any relationship is the ability to actively listen and this is no different on your first dates. One of the secrets to being charming is to be really interested in other people. This is even more the case during first dates.

Conversation should flow naturally, though you should listen more than you speak. You should ask questions about your date, their likes and dislikes and fully listen to their answers. Hopefully this will lead to discussions on those areas in which you share a mutual passion. We are not saying be passive in your conversation, but only interrupt to agree or confirm points.

To get you going, good and open-ended topics of conversation are about places you have been or want to travel to, or music, movies or books that you like. You should be willing to open up and share your feelings about people and things, but you should always avoid previous relationships at any level, you should be focused on this budding one not previously fallen ones. The level of sharing should be fun without being too intimate or needy.

Sometimes it is even best to let silence happen. It is good way to judge whether the silence is comfortable, which can indicate that you feel relaxed in each other's presence or a more awkward one, where you are searching for conversation.

Whatever the outcome of your date, you should always be interested in the other person and their life. It is not yours and therefore is interesting.

Eyes, Hands and Bodies

Before you embark on the date, make sure you are in a good positive frame of mind. If you are not in that mental state, play some music that makes you happy and positive. Put a smile on your face. These things have been shown to change your mental state the fastest.

Eye contact is important in the first date and there is a line between good, flirtatious eye contact and staring, domineering eye contact. Studies say on dates holding eye contact between 7-10 seconds at a time is about the right length.

Body language is key to any successful building of rapport, it is said that about over half of our communication is non-verbal, non-spoken. Our Bodies give us away silently. Generally, you should appear relaxed and comfortable. So as a male, keep your gestures smaller and movements slower, the person across from you is a stranger after all and you do not want to trigger their limbic system to run away! As you become more relaxed in each other's company then the gestures can get bigger, though it is best not to turn into an Over the Top Preacher!

Physical touching is intimate and can be misconstrued, if you are out and about on your date and you have to guide her, gently touch the small of her back and make sure you do not touch skin. If you are walking along, perhaps offer your arm for her to loop through. It is a chivalrous gesture without placing any pressure on the situation. (Do not forget to walk on the road-side of the pavement)

Dessert & the Bill?

Who pays the bill? Previously, this conversation would never have raised its head, but in these enlightened and equal times it does. We at the Perfect Gentleman say that the first date should be on the Gentleman, as it should adhere to our general rule that the person who does the asking should foot the bill and as we Gentlemen should have done the asking then it is up to us to pay the Bill. If there is any argument, politely insist once, but if it goes beyond that then agree to share.

The date is coming to a close and things have gone exceptionally well, now what do you do? We would say escort your date to a point of safety, her door; a cab, her car, the tube/train station and if the opportunity arises a good night kiss is sufficient. It is only a first date after all.

Some other things that have not been covered as you should already know these; A Gentleman is never late and should be early. If you are picking your date up then you should be a few minutes ahead of time.

If you have a mobile phone, unless you are expecting a family emergency, it should be on silent and not removed from your pocket for any reason except to find a location if you are lost! Your attention should be on the date and nothing else, looking at the phone will break the spell of intimacy.

Do not forget to send some kind of Thank You for your lovely evening, even if it will not go beyond that first date. The very least should be a phone call, do not text it lacks intimacy, but even better, and if the date has gone well, would be a handwritten card or note. It shows thought.

Good Luck!

Dating Beyond & Long Lasting Relationships

" I think that men know how to romance a woman and most do it well, at least for a time, otherwise women wouldn't marry them. The problem is that most of them begin to rest on their laurels. "

Nicholas Sparks

Once the first flush of the early dating is passed and you are now deep in the bloom of a growing relationship it is not the time to put your feet up in the world of romance. Relationships, like any living and breathing entity, need to be worked at, tended to, nourished and given love. It is a frequent refrain from Ladies that their Men tend to drop all the romance when a relationship becomes formed and stable. The Gentleman will always treat his partner like a person who deserves to be wooed and not just leave it to Valentines Day.

Flowers, Gifts & Poems

As the saying goes "it is the thought that counts", therefore when getting a gift, make it something that your partner wants or likes. It does not have be a grand gesture or an expensive gift, it could just be a small bunch of flowers or a hand written card with some terms of endearment.

Date Night

Make time for each other. In our modern hectic lives, we tend to run along without taking time to stop and get away from the drudgery of life. You should always be dating your partner, so regular date nights would be a great thing, even if it is just a home cooked meal.

Go Crazy

Have fun! One of the best things is make sure you laugh together. You should be best friends and best friends share jokes and have their own shorthand. Do not loose that sense of fun; occasionally do something crazy together.

Shared Experiences

One of the things that bonds us is the value of shared experiences, so make sure that the majority of these experiences are positive and special. One tip is to get a glass jar and write little notes to put in it with things that you have done either together or that you are thankful to the other person for. At the end of the year open the jar and remember together!

There is much more to a successful and happy long-term romance and marriage, but we hope this keeps you on the right path.

Marriage

The concept of Marriage dates back about 4000 years and all the way through that time has been regarded as a major life event. Take whatever time is necessary to make it as right as possible for the both of you.

This deserves a more in depth guide, for the purposes of this book here are the key points for the Perfect Romantic Gentleman and his wedding.

Marriage: The Proposal

You have taken the next step and want to commit to your partner in the act of matrimony. Firstly, can we wish you congratulations on your prospective engagement.

As with everything that we talk about here at The Perfect Gentleman, a little preparation goes a mighty long way. Start by having a very general conversation with your beloved and get a feel for what they would like. It might be flashy and grandiose or understated and refined. They might desire a grand public gesture or they might want just the two of you.

You have been with them for a while so you should have a pretty good idea. It is one of those special moments so do take the time to get it right. It will be referred to time and time again.

The Ring

There are a number of conventions that one thinks of, such as it has to be a diamond; it should cost 2-3 months salary and other such rules. As nice as these are they are just marketing ploys. Simply put, purchase a ring the lady will like and one that she will wear. If they like diamonds, get one. If they like sapphires get that. The person has to wear it for some time, so they have to be happy with it.

If you are buying it beforehand, make sure you have an accurate idea of her ring size. Take a ring of hers and get it sized, discretely. Spend what you can afford, remember expensive is not always best.

Diamonds: A Quick Guide

If you are to get a diamond then remember the four 'c's: Carat, Clarity, Colour and Cut. These factors determine the price of the gem. Carat refers to the size of the stone; the larger the stone the greater the number. Clarity is about the flaws in the stone; the greater the Clarity the more sparkle it has. Colour; the more colourless the stone the better, they are graded by letter. Cut; this can refer to the shape of the diamond, but for cost purposes it refers to the skill of the cutter of the stone.

For more on Diamonds please head to

www.theperfectgentleman.tv/BPGresources

The Setting

Pick your time and place carefully. We suggest not too intricate a plan as then there are fewer things to go wrong, but if you are doing something spectacular and worthy of that 'You Tube' moment, then put in the preparation.

Choose a venue that your partner likes and is comfortable with. If you are doing it in a large public setting be ready for applause, cheers and other forms of congratulations.

Being traditionalists here at the Perfect Gentleman, we would always get down on one knee. It has a certain element of class to it. Classic examples of locations include beaches, atop or in front of iconic buildings, and at restaurants. If you want to do something a bit different, look to weekends away, a place that they love or maybe even a bridge over a river.

Be prepared for tears; so carry a spare handkerchief or two.

The Words

We can all stumble over these on the day, simple is good. State the question confidently and clearly. Our personal favourite is "Would you do me the honour of being my wife?"

If you are more eloquent you can say more, but as it is a nervous time, simple is better!

Other Elements

Even in this day and age, it goes down very well to ask the person's parents for their child's hand. It may seem traditional but it shows a level of respect.

When you have popped the question, irrespective of asking their permission, it is correct to tell both sets of parents first, before telling your friends. Make sure the key people know before you put it out on Social Media.

In truth there is no right or wrong way to ask someone, so be brave and be daring and show your love to the world.

Marriage: Weddings

There are piles of books and magazines written about weddings, and, once you have embarked on this path, you will be taking these up to do your research. Our advice herein is taken from the Gentleman's point of View.

Get Involved

Do not sit back and let your partner do all the work. They will appreciate your input and help. It is a massive project to plan and all help will be greatly appreciated. Always engage with good humour and good taste, even if it is your fifieth venue visit. It is a special day, it should be right.

Choosing your Best Man

One of the gentleman's challenges is choosing not only a person who is your best friend but also one who can stand up and talk in front of the crowd. Think carefully about your choice and help them along the way.

Guest List

The bane of every wedding planner, bride and groom, is the Wedding Guest List. There will always be compromises and challenges. Talk at length about whom you want to invite and the budget for the wedding, as these will dictate numbers. Then if there are people that you cannot invite that are important to you, make the effort to write and explain your reasons or arrange to see or speak to them and break the news.

Venue

The choice of venue is a reflection of your tastes and style, so make sure it fits. Take a moment to think about your guests and their requirements for attending. Make sure you have all the details correct and, if you can, do at least one or two reconnaissance trips. You have to be as comfortable as possible on the day to ease any bridal nerves.

Attire

Your choice of attire will depend on the formality of the wedding you are holding. It might be the perfect time to get a Bespoke Suit for yourself, as it will make you feel excellent as well as look great.

If you are doing a more formal wedding, then we suggest hiring the Morning Suit from a specialist, as you are unlikely to use it frequently.

The Big Day

We know it will be an amazing day for you both, but it will pass in flash. As with all things, make sure you have done your preparation. Remember your speech, and remember to relax. Also, do lean on your Best Man, as that is what his role is, to support you on your big day. Enjoy the day.

The Honeymoon

The Honeymoon is that point in time when you are both together and can relax. Nowadays it is not always possible to go straight after a wedding onto your honeymoon. The Honeymoon is generally there to spend quality time together before embarking back into the normality of life, therefore make it a special trip to a destination you both want to go to.

Afterwards

There is generally a great deal to do in the aftermath of the wedding, deciding what to do with the dress, where the presents should go and all those interesting things. Do not forget to write those handwritten Thank You cards for all your guests. It will take time but is worth the effort.

This chapter just scratches the surface of what it takes to become a true Romantic Gentleman and, as with everything in the Perfect Gentleman world, it is about the learning and the journey not just the destination. Look out for a more in depth look at The Romantic Gentleman in the future.

THE JUNIOR GENTLEMAN

" The way for a young man to rise is to improve himself in every way he can, never suspecting that anybody wishes to hinder him. "

Abraham Lincoln

Introduction

In today's world of immediate access to the Internet, apps, competition to have the best mobile phone and hundreds of channels of TV telling you what the next great thing is going to be, it is sometimes hard for a young man to try to step off the path which leads to the mass clone fashions and the diluted gang speak, and instead take the path of becoming a gentleman.

Standing out in the increasingly homogenised world of fashions and social media can lead to a young man being ostracised from the crowd in a way that can leave him uncomfortable and isolated.

Our aim in this chapter of Becoming the Perfect Gentleman is to point the way onto a path where you can become a young gentleman without standing out too much from the crowd. Our aim is to educate you rather than segregate you.

If you bring some of your friends along this path with you it is highly likely that you will find that the world of a gentleman is a far more pleasant place to inhabit than the world of an apprentice gangster.

It may not mean a great deal to you at this stage of your life, but the skills that we are going to teach you will help you as you move out of the closeted world of school, college or university and, hopefully, into the world of work and life.

If you read the daily papers or watch the news you cannot fail to see the impact that recent issues with the worldwide economy have had on the job prospects of many school and university leavers.

The unemployment rate among the young is at an all time high and the jobs that are available are all hugely oversubscribed. Many highly qualified graduates have to take low paid jobs just to get a start. Unpaid internships are for many the only way to make a start in the world of work with no certainty of whether or not the experience they gain is going to lead them into any permanent paying job in an area in which they are interested.

It is much harder for the young gentleman today to get a start in life and standing out from the crowd is critical. Understanding manners, the way to dress smartly, and the correct way to behave in society at large, these are essential skills for a young man to make his mark in the world.

Self-belief, Self-confidence and Self worth

You will learn as you grow that there is a fine line between self-belief and swaggering over-confidence. You need to develop a very affirming self worth and self-belief.

It is best to learn to be positive, develop a 'can do' attitude. This is a very important element of your personality. For some it may come naturally, but others may have to work at it.

Be an original rather than a clone. Do not slavishly follow fashion. Look for a role model or someone you respect and learn from them but do not be afraid to be your own person, develop your own style and your own personality. Whatever you do, do not take yourself too seriously. While there are limited options for clowns, taking yourself too seriously can be as bad. Learn to relax and evaluate social trends and do not follow every turn slavishly.

How the Young Gentleman should behave

Treat everyone equally, men and women. Do not pick on any weaknesses, either physical or in a particular area of knowledge.

Continue to learn even when you have left school or university. Read books, magazines and newspapers, scour the Internet for knowledge. Do not get bogged down in your group of friends on a social media site. Go out, learn more about the world, meet new people, have new experiences and broaden your outlook.

Be aware that as a young man you have a different way of looking at things. This may allow you to create something totally new and revolutionary, think of Steve Jobs, Richard Branson and Bill Gates, to name but a few. But be aware that many older people will find your youthful zeal and enthusiasm a threat, so tread carefully and listen to what your elders have to teach you, and then plough your own furrow.

Always play advice from other people against your own internal moral code. Just because someone is in a position of experience if you think what he or she are telling you is wrong then question and challenge it, but do so with politeness and humility.

Never be afraid to show your emotions. Holding or suppressing your emotions in is not good for you.

Speaking

It is common for young people today to pepper their speech with 'like', "well I 'like'…", and other such phrases, "went to the shops and looked for a 'like' jacket but I couldn't 'like' find anything I wanted." This may be because you need time to think or it may just be a habit you fall into because your peers do it. You may not even be aware of it, but when you are dealing with other people you will stand out. Find a way to train yourself to stop, get someone to point out every time you do it and even if you must do it with your friends find a way to switch it off when not with them.

Clear speech, a good use of language and a broad vocabulary will take you far.

Dealing with other people

Work hard on your ability to talk to and listen to other people, the art of communication is a valuable skill. Think about holding reasoned conversations, work at your general knowledge and your understanding of current affairs so that you can discuss the world. Have an opinion and be prepared to discuss and debate with your friends. Understand that a conversation is a two-way thing, not one person berating another about their point of view. Learn to listen, appraise and respond.

Be calm, collected and confident when talking to both young and older people. Find an older person who you like and respect and talk to them, ask questions, give your opinions. Learn to do this in a friendly environment and you will find it much easier when you move out into the wider world.

Spend some time focusing on learning about non-verbal communications, as a large percentage of our communication is not the words we speak. Learning about body language is an invaluable skill to master from an early age.

Know when to keep your own council

With the proliferation of social media some people feel the need to broadcast everything they do to anyone on the Internet. Be extremely circumspect with what you publish, and the pictures and information that other people publish about you. It might be fun now, but it will come back to haunt you later in life. Be aware of your privacy settings. Make sure that you would be happy for example, any prospective employer, to see everything that is visible to a public viewer on any of the social media platforms. These days, most employers will be sure to look, as will any number of other people.

Do not get involved in gossip or talking about other people and avoid people who spend their lives gossiping. Any confidences you share with them is likely to be shared with other people.

Women

As you grow up spend time in the company of girls or women of your age and all ages. Developing the ability to be comfortable in the company of the opposite sex will hold you in good stead, as you grow older. Once you are comfortable in women's company you will not need to come up with corny lines to meet women in clubs or bars, you will be able to start a normal conversation. Being comfortable with women who are your friends will open up a huge group of friends and acquaintances. Let friendships happen naturally, do not worry because when you least expect it things will happen. It should not need to be said but be equally comfortable around people of all different types of sexuality and diversity.

Do not think of sex as the aim of a relationship. Do not make it a goal or a target. Let a relationship build, let things move at their own pace and enjoy learning how to romance your partner. Removing any pressure in this way will mean that you both enjoy learning about each other. Let the relationship grow organically and you will gain the respect of women and when the time is right you will know.

The Young Gentleman at Work, School or University

Be hungry to learn, this is a hunger that will serve you well.

At school, the ability to learn and absorb information will help you grow as a person. Learn to devour the subjects that you love and embrace the challenge of the ones that are less pleasant.

When you arrive at a new job there will be an induction and then, depending on the quality of the organisation, there will be a training program set up to teach you about the company and your job. If you work for a large organisation it is likely that there will be huge amounts of information available on an intranet, which offers the opportunity for self-learning.

Hunt out information, use it and focus on educating yourself over and above what your school or the company gives you. Do not make a big thing of this, just get your head down and work. No one likes a show off so it is better to learn, absorb the information and improve yourself steadily and slowly.

Think hard about other skills, which will help to do your job or make school life easier. Most people will need to use Microsoft packages such as Word, Excel or PowerPoint, but very few people have ever had formal training. Look for ways to improve your skills here and think about touch-typing skills if you have never been taught how to properly use a keyboard. All hugely valuable and transferable skills for the modern world.

Work hard, but be smart about it. Whether it is at school or when you get a job, whether it is an internship or your first proper job, give it 100%. Work hard, but make sure you work to live rather than live to work. In the working world, this is especially true, early in your working life you will be pressured to work long hours and there can be the hidden threat that there are a huge number of people who would love your job.

Set yourself a limit and stick to it. There is always likely to be a panic or a special project so try to monitor the numbers of hours you work each week or each month and make sure you stick within a few percent of that figure. There is no point burning yourself out, you will end up doing a poor job and having no private life at all.

Always go into a job, a project, or that piece of coursework, with a clear view of where you want to go and how you want to get there. It may sound strange but every time you enter a new job, or situation, you should go in thinking about where it is going to take you and what your next move is. This will not only colour the way you behave in your new job or in the university, but also help you set your own personal rules that you will work to.

Always have a plan in mind. It may change over the period you are there, but always have a plan.

When you have achieved the status, the goals, the level of experience or the learning you set yourself do not get stuck, do not be afraid to start to look for the next step wherever that maybe.

Keep going, and do not give up. Be persistent, if something is worth doing then it is worth working at. Do not give up when the first difficulty is presented. Work out a way round obstacles and move on. Do not worry if you take more time than other people, you are learning, keep striving, always do your best.

Find a mentor to help and advise you. Many companies and universities will have formal mentoring programmes for employees/ students, and, if they do, find a mentor you respect to work with on your development. If your company/university does not have a formal programmes, then seek out someone who you respect and do not be afraid to ask them if they will help to mentor you. Most people will be flattered to be asked and will help.

Diet and Fitness

Diet is not something you think about when you are a young man, as the temptations of fast food and sweets abound. Though acquiring a good knowledge of food and what makes or constitutes a healthy diet is essential. We are becoming a world plagued with obesity. This is due to the proliferation of sugar rich foods, the fact that we can eat what we want and when we like, and because we do not exert ourselves as physically as we once did.

We suggest that as a Young Gentleman you should learn to cook as this will give you a good knowledge of food and give you the ability to make healthy food for yourself, and then you can have that slice of cake without worrying.

Fitness is essential to a happy and long life and as a young man there are plenty of opportunities and the time to indulge in your favourite sporting activity. It is a habit that one should not forget as one gets older. Even if you are not a 'sporty' type, exercise is good for you and even walking has been proved to be hugely beneficial.

The Perfect Gentleman has a mantra about being able to defend oneself and others when the situation arises. The martial tradition is long linked to the Gentleman and that should not be overlooked. We believe that it breeds discipline, skill, determination, fitness and self-confidence alongside its more practical applications.

The Ability to Look After Yourself

At the Perfect Gentleman we have huge respect for Bartitsu, the Gentleman's Martial Art.

Bartitsu is a martial art developed by E.W. Barton-Wright, an English Gentleman, who was by training an engineer not a professional fighter. He lived and worked in Japan between 1885 and 1898. He was among the first Europeans known to have studied the Japanese martial arts, and was almost certainly the first to have taught them in Europe, the British Empire or the Americas.

Comparatively little is known about the period that Barton-Wright spent living in Kobe, Japan. Arriving during mid-1895, he spent the next several years supervising an antimony smelting operation for E.H. Hunter and Company, a large manufacturing business. Most of his free time was apparently spent training at the Shinden Fudo Ryu jiujitsu dojo of his sensei, Terajima Kuniichiro.

In 1898, Barton-Wright returned to England and announced the formation of a "New Art of Self Defence". This art, he claimed, combined the best elements of a range of fighting styles into a unified whole, which he had named Bartitsu. Barton-Wright had previously also studied "boxing, wrestling, fencing, savate and the use of the stiletto under recognised masters", reportedly testing his skills by "engaging toughs (street fighters) until (he) was satisfied in their application." He defined Bartitsu as meaning "self defence in all its forms"; the word was a portmanteau of his own surname and of "Jujitsu". In effect it was the world's first modern mixed martial art.

Bartitsu would have faded away if Sir Arthur Conan Doyle had not mentioned it in his Sherlock Holmes novels (even though it was misspelt) as the famous detective's martial art. In fact, it was used by Robert Downey Jnr in the recent movie adaptations.

As with all Martial Arts, it was more about prevention than aggression. In his notes for a lecture delivered to the Japan Society of London in 1901, Barton-Wright wrote:

Keeping safe / Self Protection

Be proactive

Based on awareness and avoidance

Simple effective principles

Three Golden Rules

Be responsible – Take individual responsibility for your own safety

Be realistic – Take realistic security precautions

Be Aware – The cornerstone of self protection

As our great friend James Marwood, one of the world's top practitioners of the art, says;

"Be aware of the three **STUPIDS** - going to stupid places with stupid people and doing stupid things"

To learn more about Bartitsu and to find a local club near you or indeed any other Martial Art go to our resources website for this book - www.theperfectgentleman.tv/BPGresources.

The Junior Gentleman is embarking on a journey and will need all the assistance he can get and we hope to be here to help.

CONCLUSION

Thank you, you have made it through this book with us and we hope you have enjoyed it, learnt a few things and are hungry to continue your journey to Becoming the Perfect Gentleman.

We have endeavoured to provide a comprehensive overview of some of the core areas that we believe make up a gentleman. We know we have had to omit a great deal and not covered in detail all the aspects that we would have liked in this book, for this we apologise but we will keep on adding to this and other aspects of the Perfect Gentleman world over the course of time.

The Skills

Becoming the Perfect Gentleman is about learning and eventually perhaps mastering a set of skills, for everything can be taught and we hope to teach you it all.

The skills in this book and indeed throughout the Perfect Gentleman world, have been perfected by experts and can be practiced and mastered.

So please go out, have fun and learn, it is always about the Journey and never the destination, as even we here who have written this book are always learning to be a better Gentleman.

Advancing with The Perfect Gentleman

We at the Perfect Gentleman are here to fulfill our mission and therefore we are here to help you in your journey. We realise that books are not the only medium to help you learn and we could only cram a few items into these pages.

We run our signature 2-day event, Becoming The Perfect Gentleman, at a city near you. This experiential event will include the core content but in an exciting, experiential way, taught by experts and with engaging surprises, such as delivering a live wet shave on stage.

We have launched our series of Short Courses in London, but will be expanding them around the world. These include 'How to Pick the Perfect Suit', 'How to be Charming' and 'How to have the Perfect 1st Date'.

We are building our content on a daily basis with our Code of the Gentleman magazine (www.codeofthegentleman.com) our plans are simple; we intend to delve into more details in all aspects of the Gentleman and share it with you.

This Book was an overview and we want to delve deeper into more aspects of the gentleman, therefore we are planning a series of books with more information in each. The first in this series will be Becoming the Stylish Gentleman, which covers in more detail all manner of dress from Suits, formal wear and being a gentleman in various different climates.

Then we intend to work on Becoming the Romantic Gentleman. This will cover everything about how to find, woo and keep the woman of your dreams. We will include everything from how to prepare and deliver the perfect date, how to cook a fantastic romantic meal, pick an amazing bunch of flowers and how to keep the romance alive.

Sign up now to our newsletter on the website (www.theperfectgentleman.tv) to get the latest information.

We look forward to having you on this journey with us as we endeavour to make the world a more respectful, stylish and Gentlemanly place, one man at a time and the next man will be…

You!

THE PERFECT GENTLEMAN'S MANIFESTO

We, Gentlemen of the world, agree it is time to stand up and be counted. To build a better society, founded on long standing principles that have guided civilisation for over a thousand years.

We believe it is time to bring back grace, courage and integrity. Once again establishing the Gentleman, as the champion of the good, the pillar of honesty and the guardian of honour.

We will endeavour to educate all men to these guiding principles :

First, we must **Respect** *ourselves, creating the solid foundation upon which we can grow.*

We awaken **Confidence** *within ourselves, so that others may look to our example and we may lead the way.*

We are **Determined** *to succeed, in all aspects of our lives.*

We seek **Knowledge***, as a gentleman realises that to grow as a man he must feed his mind as well as nourish his body.*

The Gentleman will be strong, unearthing his **Masculinity** *so that he may defend himself and others when the need arises.*

The Second level is to have Respect for all our fellow humans, showing appreciation for those around you.

*Being **Stylish** is an external presentation of our impeccable convictions.*

*We embrace **Chivalry**, showing respect, courtesy and good manners, in all our dealings with every person.*

*With **Charm** we ease our interactions with others and make the world a more pleasant place.*

*We believe gentlemen succeed by cultivating **Humility**, rather than the pretensions of ego.*

---

*The Third and final level, we have **Respect** for the world at large and realise that all our actions have an impact.*

*In life **Courage** armours us, to face our fears, adversities and challenges.*

*A gentleman has **Honour** in all his words, deeds and endeavours.*

*With **Loyalty**, we forge bonds that make us stronger than we are alone.*

*A gentleman must show **Compassion** in all his dealings, striving to help those who cannot always help themselves.*

The gentleman will rise again and we will discover courage to live these values, the integrity to not be swayed and the grace to show others the way.

If you identify with these values, stand with us as we endeavour to take each step on this journey to become the Perfect Gentleman

ZACH FALCONER-BARFIELD

Zach's mother and grandmother raised him to be a gentleman and he thanks them daily for this service. After being asked a number of times to help female friends with their partners and being extremely frustrated with the lack of manners on the streets, he decided to launch The Perfect Gentleman. He is the 1st Gentleman at the company and writes regularly for the Magazine and is the lead trainer.

He is an entrepreneur, lecturer, writer and gentleman. As a serial entrepreneur, Zach started selling to his classmates at school. He has been involved with the creation of more than eleven businesses.

Zach has an MBA from Cass Business School, and is a Master NLP Practitioner and Coach. He is a trained actor having attended Arts Educational School in London.

Nic Wing

As our Editor in Chief and Second Gentleman, Nic is the safe pair of hands at the helm, guiding our gentleman through the mass of information they will acquire. Nic started his career in sales for a large multinational organization but left to pursue his passions.

Nic is the creator of The London Cigar Guide App, which will guide you to London's finest cigar stores and cigar terraces. He organises trips to Havana and cigar training for a Mayfair cigar Store. He is also a journalist and copywriter, having written for a number of magazines and websites on all manner of gentlemanly subjects.

Lightning Source UK Ltd.
Milton Keynes UK
UKOW03f0609150714

235135UK00001B/11/P